# Dairy-Free Cookbook

**How to Order:**
Quantity discounts are available from the publisher, Prima Publishing & Communications, P.O. Box 1260JZ, Rocklin, CA 95677; telephone (916) 624-5718. On your letterhead include information concerning the intended use of the books and the number of books you wish to purchase.

*U.S. Bookstores and Libraries:* Please submit all orders to St. Martin's Press, 175 Fifth Avenue, New York, NY 10010; telephone (212) 674-5151.

# Dairy-Free Cookbook

## Jane Zukin

**Prima Publishing & Communications**
P.O. Box 1260JZ
Rocklin, CA 95677
(916) 624-5718

Production by Robin Lockwood, Bookman Productions
Typography by R. Nolan & Sons
Interior design by Judith Levinson
Jacket design by The Dunlavey Studio

Prima Publishing & Communications
Rocklin, CA

Library of Congress Cataloging-in-Publication Data

Zukin, Jane.
  Dairy-free cookbook/Jane Zukin
  p.      cm.
  Includes index.
  ISBN 0-914629-88-3 : $18.95
  1. Milk-free diet—Recipes.   2. Lactose intolerance—Diet therapy.
3. Vegetarian cookery.   I. Title
RM234.5.Z83   1989                                                 89-3921

89 90 91 92   **RRD**   10 9 8 7 6 5 4 3 2 1

Printed in the United States of America

*Dedicated to my father, Samuel Shetzer*

# RECOGNITION OF LACTOSE INTOLERANCE

. . . the important point is to recognize that milk is not a food that everybody "needs" or automatically accepts. With regard to management, once lactose intolerance is suspected in a patient, the symptoms usually disappear with elimination of the offending disaccharide. While most lactose intolerant individuals will still be able to tolerate milk in cereal or coffee, it should be remembered that some may be bothered by as little as three ounces; some patients do best if they avoid ice-cold milk, or, drink milk with a meal. Symptoms of an underlying disease (ulcerative colitis, irritable colon syndrome) may continue, but often in a less severe form if lactose intolerance is only one of the patient's problems. In general, most persons who have had symptoms of intolerance are markedly improved once they know of the connection between their symptoms and milk ingestion. Some, indeed, are quite pleased to learn that their problem, which may have been previously dismissed as a neurotic manifestation, enjoys the status of an enzyme deficiency."

Theodore Bayless, M.D.
Foremost authority on lactose intolerance
Johns Hopkins University

# CONTENTS

# FOREWORD

Milk, whole or as a component of processed foods, is a dietary staple of most societies. It is a major source of nutrients such as protein and calcium. Besides, who can resist the cool refreshing taste of milk? Unfortunately, milk contains a sugar called lactose. Most of us gradually lose the ability to digest lactose as we grow older. Occasionally, infants develop lactose intolerance or even acquire an allergy to milk protein. When the dietary load of lactose exceeds our digestive capacity, physical disturbances result. These symptoms may include abdominal distention, intestinal cramping, diarrhea, and excess gas. Millions of people suffer with disorders such as these. Many of them, however, are unaware that they are milk intolerant. It is hard to believe that something as "wholesome" as milk can make you sick. Moreover, the cause of the symptoms is sometimes difficult to identify because distress may arise from the ingestion of food products which contain lactose as a hidden ingredient.

In principle, treatment of lactose intolerance is simple. Reduce the dietary intake of the offending sugar. But what can you eat if you are extremely sensitive to lactose and live in a society where milk is everywhere and in everything? Read Jane Zukin's book!

Jane Zukin, for the first time, has put together an authoritative reference source for the milk sufferer. *Dairy-Free Cookbook* does indeed provide easy-to-follow, delicious, milk-free recipes. However, the book contains much more. There is valuable, factual information regarding the cause and treatment of this disorder. You can also learn what foods or products should be avoided in a grocery store or in a restaurant. Useful tables are provided such as that which summarizes the lactose content of various foods. The author has done a great service by writing a book designed to help people help themselves. So, lean back, relax, learn about lactose intolerance and . . . bon appetit.

Joel V. Weinstock, M.D.
Department of Internal Medicine
Director, Division of Gastroenterology
University of Iowa

# INTRODUCTION

Writers are supposed to write about what they know. It helps their credibility and stirs their passion, therefore making the prose more eloquent and significant. Well, if anyone can be passionate about cow's milk, I certainly can. I know the subject well, having raised three children on a milk-free diet, then succumbing to complete lactose intolerance myself ten years ago after months of viral enteritis complicated by hyperthyroidism. The questions I had about lactose intolerance and milk allergy prompted me to learn as much as I could about these conditions and their management because in my house, dealing with the subject was an everyday occurrence.

Eighteen years ago my oldest son was born. David became ill within twelve days. He was in pain, had non-stop diarrhea, and projectile vomiting. Many tests were done to try and identify a bacterial infection, but to no avail. He was also checked for cystic fibrosis but was free from that diagnosis. Eventually, after several weeks, David was put on a soy-based formula. I remember his first feeding well because, although it sounds impossible, he accepted his new formula eagerly, as if he knew that we were finally aware of the proper solution to his problem. He relaxed his tense body, accepted the nipple without thrusting his tongue, and began to nurse peacefully as if to say, "Thanks, Mom." We were all amazed.

Sixteen months later, Eric was born. He went on soy formula when he was nine days old. Three years afterward when Renee was born, she was fed soy formula from the start. At the time, it was somewhat difficult to accept intolerance to milk, because then, many pediatricians were uninformed regarding lactose intolerance and milk allergy. While the products were available, soy formula had to be specially ordered from the pharmacy. That's quite a departure from the infant-formula marketplace today. Then, it was generally thought that changing infant formulas quickly was unwise. Besides, not drinking milk was akin to being unpatriotic and smacked of promoting unhealthy eating habits, something parents were reluctant to do.

Ten years ago, I became lactose intolerant as a result of viral enteritis. It is not uncommon to lose certain enzymes during this kind of illness, but I was left with lasting enzyme depletion because my condition was complicated by hyperthyroidism, something that contributed to more serious digestive distress. I needed to eliminate all forms of dairy products and lactose from my diet completely, and probably forever. Then I really had a problem. While the kids ate peanut butter, I longed for "adult" foods like creamed soups and mousse, and dip for the crudités. So I looked for milk-free cookbooks and combed the library stacks for information about lactose intolerance and milk allergy. The search didn't yield much.

Eventually, I wrote my own book, *The Milk-Free Diet Cookbook*, which was published in 1982. The letters I received from readers all across the country were grateful ones, and I still communicate with some of those people today. We share information and commiserate with one another, but mostly marvel at how the world has changed for those of us who have to give up milk. Now, the marketplace is full of exciting new milk-free products, and the research is yielding important information about the genetic factors of lactose intolerance and the huge numbers of people affected by it. Soy infant formulas are in every supermarket and corner drugstore, and the possibility of switching formulas is met with much less resistance by pediatricians.

A new book, this book, was necessary in order to update the scientific information, and report on the new products in the marketplace. Lactose-enzyme products have become more reliable, and good processing has advanced enough to make lactose-free and milk protein-free cheeses obtainable. We now know that lactose intolerance is normal for the older adult, and that 40 percent of children with recurrent pain syndrome (RAP) are lactose intolerant. We are no longer startled by people on a special diet such as this one, because in the last fifteen years, food management has come to play a greater role in the medical arena, and health-conscious people make food concessions all the time.

In response to a growing awareness, I began publishing *The Newsletter for People with Lactose Intolerance and Milk Allergy* in 1986. *The Newsletter* reports medical information and product information and offers readers the opportunity to communicate with one another in a nationwide support group. There is a section in *The Newsletter* for advice from experts and even a department devoted especially to the needs of infants and children. Not surprisingly, readers are grateful for the opportunity to exchange ideas and brainstorm solutions to problems. For me, it has meant much satisfaction.

I love milk. It makes the Cheerios float and the Oreos melt, and is really the only suitable thing to wash down chocolate cake. Don't think I'm not jealous of those who can be comfortable milk drinkers, I wish I could be one. But for millions of people in the world, a milk-free diet will have to do. I hope this book helps you to enjoy a rich lifestyle despite the elimination of diary foods and that the information helps to allay your fears. I hope the food ideas excite your palate and that you use this book until the binding breaks, realizing that each time you do, you will feel a little more secure.

A heartfelt thank you goes out to *The Newsletter* readers who give me so much encouragement and willingly share their wonderful food ideas. Thank you to my mother—the real cook in the family who can always think of a wonderful substitute for cream cheese—and to my friends for always serving at least one thing I can eat. Through all of this I have learned that people are much more important than food, but when both are terrific, everything goes down smoothly.

# 1

# Giving Up Milk

I t's hard to believe that milk, so shrouded in love,
nurturing, and goodness, can adversely affect so many
people. Yet it is estimated that the majority of the people
in the world cannot properly digest milk and, as a result,
may suffer digestive distress in varying degrees of intensity. I
realize this may be difficult for many people to accept, since,
especially in our culture, milk is a food we've been raised to
revere. It builds our bones and our teeth and soothes our
insomnia. Milk strengthens us with muscle-building protein.
We fortify milk with vitamin D so that we're enriched with its
properties of "bottled sunshine," and we boast about its presence in junk food, as if the addition of milk somehow elevates its
stature. We rationalize that if it has milk in it, it must be okay.

But okay for whom? Certainly not okay for the 50 million
Americans who are lactose intolerant. They will experience
bloating, abdominal pain, and diarrhea after drinking milk. It is
definitely not okay for the majority of Blacks, Jews, Greeks,
Eskimos, and American Indians, although thousands suffer
needlessly because either they or their physicians are reluctant to
give up the milk in their diet. Studies prove that older people
cannot drink milk or tolerate other dairy products as well as

they may have during their youth because we all lose some of the ability to digest the lactose in milk as we age. It's a natural part of the aging process.

Milk is hardly okay for infants and children who are allergic to its protein. They will suffer respiratory distress, including stuffiness, mucous buildup, wheezing, or asthma. With some of these allergic children, skin rashes or eczema will appear. Milk has long been identified as the most common allergen among infants and children under age three, but to look at our cultural habits, that would be hard to confirm. Parents are undauntingly faithful to milk. It is a staple of American life and an abiding part of childhood. Even the parents of milk-allergic children cling to the hope that their child's condition will be short-lived.

Some adults have a difficult time in the beginning. All their lives they've been told that milk is necessary, and now, how will they manage without it? The prescription to give up milk and dairy products is usually met with anxiety and anguish. People worry about their calcium intake. They worry about their protein intake. They feel a loss when asked to give up foods they love. But the truth is, we weren't necessarily meant to drink cow's milk in the first place, which is why many people and all other mammals have a physical intolerance to it.

We were designed to drink milk only through our earliest years until weaned, and we were meant to drink the milk of our mothers, not that of cows. Stop and think about it. We don't see baby goats suckling from pigs. We don't see lambs growing into sheep and still nursing. And yet, particularly in western cultures, we urge our children to drink the milk of cows and teach them to continue to do so throughout their adult lives. This cultural influence is the result of the lifestyles of dairying societies that became part of our history 10,000 years ago, and we're faithful to it until this day.

Many of us are incapable of digesting the quantity of milk American cultural standards mandate. In order to digest the lactose in milk (milk sugar), we must have sufficient amounts of the enzyme lactase in our intestine. When the lactase enzyme is reduced, or the lactose level is increased beyond our enzyme activity, malabsorption takes place and symptoms ensue. Our lactase level is quite high at birth, permitting us to be nursed by our mothers, whose milk contains large amounts of lactose. A significant drop occurs between two and five years of age, generally leveling off until the time between our teen and middle adult years. Slowly, our lactase enzyme activity diminishes as we age, and dairy products become problematic once again. This pattern has been passed along genetically with the exception of a mutation scientists identify which enables some people, mostly western European dairying cultures and their descendants, to continue to be milk drinkers throughout adulthood. That's right. Scientists consider milk tolerance a mutation and milk intolerance the norm. Therefore, it is not unusual to be sensitive to milk; it's unusual to be able to digest it.

If you previously thought that giving up milk and all other dairy products placed you in the minority, alone and deprived, think again. Milk is a problem for many people in a variety of situations, including:

infants with transient diarrhea caused by flu or teething

children and adults with IBD—inflammatory bowel disease—including ulcerative colitis and Crohn's disease (ileitis)

people who have stomach upsets caused by antibiotics or antacids with magnesia, laxatives, colchicine, quinidine compounds

children with celiac disease, corresponding to non-tropical sprue in adults

travelers who experience diarrhea as a result of different food and water

premature infants whose lactase enzyme levels are not high enough

infants born with galactosemia

surgical patients who have had areas of intestine removed

men and women who are working to reduce the saturated fats in their diet

people who are recovering from parasitic or bacterial diseases like giardia or salmonella.

None of this means that giving up milk will be easy, however. As you will learn, milk in some form or other is present in hundreds of thousands of foods, medicines, candies, baked goods, meats, vitamin tablets, prescription drugs, . . . the list goes on. From experience, I can assure you that, once accepted and understood, a dairy-free diet can be filled with a complete array of nourishing and even "creamy" foods. By giving up milk you will be giving up a major source of saturated fat in the diet. And because so many processed foods are made with milk or lactose, you will be forced to eat more fresh and homemade foods. The benefits of this are obvious.

# 2

# Is It Lactose Intolerance?

## WHAT IS LACTOSE?

Simply put, lactose is milk sugar. It is a disaccharide—a double sugar—composed of glucose and galactose. Lactose is only found in the milk of animals. It is not found naturally in fruits or vegetables or meats. It is *not* sucrose, or dextrose, or fructose. Lactose is the carbohydrate of animal milk, including human milk, which, incidentally, contains almost twice as much lactose as cow's milk. Often, prepared infant formulas have added lactose to make the cow's milk resemble human milk as much as possible.

## WHAT IS LACTOSE INTOLERANCE?

Lactose intolerance is the inability to properly digest the lactose in milk. Lactose is split into its two component sugars by the enzyme *lactase* located in the small intestine. From there, the liver changes the galactose into glucose and it moves on into the bloodstream to supply the cells with fuel for energy. If the enzyme *lactase* is not active enough, or if the amount of milk ingested is too great for the amount of *lactase*, or if there is a depletion of the enzyme, complete digestion of lactose cannot take place. Unabsorbed lactose remains in the small intestine for an extended period. Within a couple of hours, the lactose is carried to the colon, where it becomes fermented by intestinal bacteria. It is this fermentation that causes the unpleasant symptoms of lactose intolerance.

Lactose intolerance was first identified by pediatricians in 1901, but until the late 1950s, studies on the subject were obscure or non-existent. Then, interest peaked once again and important work began to take place. Lactose intolerance is now definable and manageable in several categories.

## Primary Lactose Intolerance

This is the most common type of lactose intolerance seen among children and adults. It is a normal, age-related decrease in lactase enzyme activity. Primary lactose intolerance is hereditary, passed on by an autosomal recessive gene. Levels of intolerance vary for each individual. Some experimentation should take place so that people are aware of their own digestive capabilities.

## Secondary Lactose Intolerance

This is most likely a transient disorder that affects infants, children, and adults. It occurs when external or infective factors influence the working of the intestinal mucosa. It is a consequence of flare-ups of other gastrointestinal diseases like Crohn's or ulcerative colitis. It may be caused by celiac disease or viral diarrhea. Most likely, when the causative disorder is cleared up, the activity of the lactase enzyme will resume. So children and adults bothered by an episode of diarrhea should eliminate milk and other dairy products for a while. Later, when they are feeling better, dairy products can be eaten once again. Sometimes enzyme depletion from other causes is permanent, particularly among adults, who then may not be able to reintroduce dairy foods to their diet.

# Alactasia

Alactasia is another name for "congenital lactose intolerance." Since lactose is present in mother's milk, being born without the ability to digest it would be inconsistent with life itself. Yet it does happen. Infants who have symptoms of alactasia need to be treated immediately because prolonged diarrhea may cause failure to thrive or fatal dehydration.

# Galactosemia

Galactosemia is a birth defect classified as an "inborn error of metabolism." It is caused by the absence or abnormality of an enzyme required to convert galactose to glucose. Since galactose is *only* found as a by-product of lactose digestion, all sources of lactose must be eliminated from the diet. Infants born with galactosemia begin vomiting, have diarrhea, and are quite lethargic within a week of their birth. There may be an enlarged spleen, liver damage, and cataracts. This child fails to gain weight and becomes malnourished. If left untreated, galactosemia is a serious disorder that renders the child mentally retarded and likely to die. However, when properly treated after early detection, children born with galactosemia may not suffer dread reactions and are likely to have minimal, if any, damage to the brain.

## WHAT ARE THE SYMPTOMS OF LACTOSE INTOLERANCE?

Symptoms and their severity vary from person to person. Generally, people with lactose intolerance will have abdominal pain, gas, cramping, a bloated feeling, and diarrhea. There may even be distension of the abdominal area. Prolonged diarrhea brings with it side effects such as rectal tenderness, bodily weakness, dehydration, and weight loss. These symptoms may be noted within an hour after ingesting milk or other dairy products, or they can occur several days later, after the accumulation of poorly digested material. Some people have tolerable discomfort, others are quite ill or may even have to be hospitalized. Though the degree of intensity of symptoms is enormous, abdominal distress is the common denominator.

## MAKING THE DIAGNOSIS

There are several ways to confirm the diagnosis of lactose intolerance. The simplest is a self-test easily done at home. If you suspect lactose intolerance, eliminate all milk and dairy products from your diet for two weeks. Then drink a full glass of milk and wait to see if symptoms recur. If not, you may want to try another glass to see what happens. If you feel gassy or bloated or develop diarrhea, you have obviously exceeded your threshold for lactose.

Your doctor may want to run stool cultures to rule out bacterial infection or an intestinal parasite. Then you may be asked to have a Lactose Tolerance Test or a Hydrogen Breath Test, the two most commonly administered test procedures to confirm the lactose intolerance diagnosis. Be aware that if you are lactose intolerant, both of these test procedures will make you uncomfortable because each requires that you drink a pint or so of sweetened lemonade or similar beverage loaded with 50 grams of lactose.

## Lactose Tolerance Test

This is the oldest test used to confirm a lactose intolerance diagnosis. It was routinely used for adults and now has been adapted to testing children as well. Patients drink a large amount of a sweet drink carrying a 50-gram lactose load. In the body, when lactose is ingested, the lactase enzyme acts upon it and breaks it down into glucose and galactose. From there, the liver changes the galactose into glucose. If this happens properly, the glucose then travels into the bloodstream and elevates the fasting glucose level. If absorption is incomplete, the blood glucose level does not rise accordingly, and lactose intolerance is confirmed.

In practical terms, what this means to you is that after fasting for a specified length of time, you will have your blood drawn to measure the glucose level. Then you will drink the lactose beverage. Blood will be drawn periodically over two hours to measure the glucose level. No rise in glucose level, no absorption of lactose. Generally, the uncomfortable effects of the lactose will show within that time as well, so be prepared for digestive distress.

# Hydrogen Breath Test

As its name suggests, this test measures the amount of hydrogen in the breath. Normally, we have no hydrogen in our breath. But hydrogen is produced by bacteria in the colon when it receives an undigested carbohydrate like lactose. The undigested lactose is fermented into various gases, hydrogen being one of them. Hydrogen is absorbed from the intestines and is carried through the bloodstream to the lungs. Here the gas is exhaled. Therefore, hydrogen in the breath means undigested lactose in the gut. To ensure the accuracy of the test, patients must not eat other foods that may cause excessive gas production: cabbage, brussels sprouts, or beans. The patient must not take any antibiotics, which kill the fermenting bacteria, and must not have recently used any laxatives or enemas. In addition, chronic diarrhea that eliminates too much of the normal bacteria in the colon can alter the test results. Smoking also interferes with the test's accuracy.

The process goes like this: You exhale and your breath is analyzed. You drink the lactose-loaded beverage and have your breath analyzed at regular intervals. Naturally, if you are lactose intolerant you will have digestive distress symptoms during the test.

# Stool Acidity Test

Giving a lactose load to a baby may be dangerous due to the threatening possibility of prolonged diarrhea and ensuing dehydration. Therefore, the usual measurement tests for older children and adults are not done for infants. Many pediatricians simply recommend a change from cow's milk to soy formula and watch for symptoms to abate. Sometimes a Stool Acidity Test will be done. This test measures the amount of acid in the stool, because undigested lactose in the colon that is fermented by bacteria will create lactic acid and other short-chain fatty acids. Also, glucose may be present in the stool sample as a result of unabsorbable lactose in the colon. Testing stool samples in this manner obviously presents no danger to infants or very young children.

There are other ways of measuring lactose malabsorption, including a Galactose Test, a Carbon Dioxide Radioisotope Breath Test, Urine Testing, even Biopsy, but their use is not as popular as the others described.

## WHAT IS THE TREATMENT
## FOR LACTOSE INTOLERANCE?

Once the diagnosis is made, immediate elimination of lactose is essential. You must stop eating all milk products, including cheese, yogurt, sour cream, ice cream, butter, margarine, and cottage cheese. If you have had diarrhea, help yourself by drinking lots of liquids for rehydration. Drink water, clear juice, and broth. Don't eat fried foods or other foods that are difficult for you to digest easily. Prepare steamed vegetables and fruits, broiled fish or poultry, and limit the number of eggs you eat, due to their high fat content, which causes indigestion in many people. Later, you will learn how to experiment with small amounts of dairy products to find your lactose tolerance level.

Look for lactose on the labels of prepared foods and on the packages of over-the-counter vitamins and other medications you are taking. Read every label of every item you purchase in the supermarket, and if lactose is listed in the ingredients, leave it on the shelf. Also, you may not have foods that contain whey, dried milk, acidophilus milk, nonfat milk, or milk in any other form. *IF IT SAYS MILK, IT IS MILK.* You may be able to have milk proteins, but for now, please avoid them. Milk proteins are: casein, sodium caseinate, lactalbumin, and lactoglobulin. You may experiment with these later.

If you have been uncomfortable for a while, give yourself permission to relax and mend. Your physician may prescribe a mild medication to slow down and calm your digestive system. Try to ease the pressure in your life, reduce stress, avoid caffeine and smoking, eliminate all alcoholic drinks, and spend the next few weeks getting stronger.

## FINDING YOUR LACTOSE TOLERANCE LEVEL

Once you have sufficiently eliminated all forms of lactose from your diet, you should see results in a matter of days, with optimum effects occurring after a few weeks. At this time, you may begin to experiment with small amounts of foods that contain milk. Start with breads and cereals and other baked goods that are prepared with milk. Try something, wait a day, try it again. If symptoms don't occur, move ahead. Continue with dairy products that are fermented like yogurt, or have low lactose levels like aged cheeses. Finally, experimentation with milk may take place, starting with very small amounts and perhaps working up to one cup per day. Many people can tolerate milk at this level. Some can only have milk in a fermented form. Some people can't have milk at all.

## TABLE 1

### WHO IS LACTOSE INTOLERANT?

| CULTURE | PERCENT LACTOSE INTOLERANT |
|---|---|
| Africans | 93% |
| American Indians | 83% |
| Arabs | 80% |
| Black Americans | 70% |
| Caucasian Americans | 8% |
| Danish | 3% |
| Eastern European Jews | 78% |
| Eskimos | 88% |
| Filipinos | 95% |
| Finns | 19% |
| Greeks | 87% |
| Indians | 56% |
| Israeli Jews | 60% |
| Japanese | 92% |
| Mexicans | 60% |
| South Americans | 65% |

Source: Wisconsin Department of Health and Social Services
Nutrition Newsletter for Consultant Dieticians #3-78
July, August, September 1978. Studies done by Dr. Theodore Bayless

### Table 2

### LACTOSE CONTENT OF VARIOUS FOODS

| PRODUCT | UNIT | GMS. LACTOSE |
|---|---|---|
| *Milks* | | |
| Buttermilk | 1 cup | 9-11 |
| Chocolate Milk | 1 cup | 10-12 |
| Dried Whole Milk | 1 cup | 48 |
| Eggnog | 1 cup | 14 |

| PRODUCT | UNIT | GMS. LACTOSE |
|---|---|---|
| Evaporated Milk | 1 cup | 20 |
| Goat's Milk | 1 cup | 9.4 |
| Human Milk | 1 cup | 13.8 |
| Lowfat Milk | 1 cup | 9-13 |
| Low-Sodium Milk | 1 cup | 9 |
| Nonfat Dry Milk | 1 cup | 40 |
| Skim Milk | 1 cup | 12-14 |
| Sweetened Condensed Milk | 1 cup | 35 |
| Whole Milk | 1 cup | 11 |
| *Miscellaneous Dairy Foods* | | |
| Butter | 1 tsp | .06 |
| Butter | 2 pats | .10 |
| Half and Half | 1 TBS | 0.6 |
| Light Cream | 1 TBS | 0.6 |
| Lowfat Yogurt | 1 cup | 10-15 |
| Margarine | 1 tsp | .90 |
| Sour Cream | ½ cup | 3.2 |
| *Cheeses* | | |
| American Processed Cheese | 1 ounce | .50 |
| Blue Cheese | 1 ounce | .70 |
| Camembert | 1 ounce | .10 |
| Cheddar | 1 ounce | .50 |
| Colby | 1 ounce | .70 |
| Cottage Cheese | 1 cup | 5-6 |
| Cream Cheese | 1 ounce | .80 |
| Dry Curd Cottage Cheese | 1 cup | 2 |
| Gouda | 1 ounce | .60 |
| Limburger | 1 ounce | .10 |
| Lowfat Cottage Cheese | 1 cup | 7 |

*(Continued on next page)*

| PRODUCT | UNIT | GMS. LACTOSE |
|---------|------|--------------|
| Parmesan | 1 ounce | .80 |
| Pimento Processed | 1 ounce | .50-1.70 |
| Swiss | 1 ounce | .50 |
| *Desserts* | | |
| Fudge Bar | 1 | 4.9 |
| Ice Cream Sandwich | 1 | 2.4 |
| Ice Cream (Vanilla) | 1 cup | 9 |
| Ice Milk (Vanilla) | 1 cup | 10 |
| Orange Cream Bar | 1 | 3.1 |
| Orange Sherbet | 1 cup | 4 |
| Soft Ice Cream (Vanilla) | 1 cup | 9 |
| Whipped Cream (Heavy) | ½ cup | 3.1 |
| Whipped Cream (Light) | 1 TBS | 0.4 |

Sources: American Journal of Clinical Nutrition
Volume 31 #4 April 1987, J.D. Welsh

Michigan State University Nutrient Bank & Sealtest Foods
1984 reprinted in Milk-Sugar Dilemma by Martens & Martens

# 3

# Is It Milk Allergy?

## WHAT IS MILK ALLERGY?

There are debatable issues dealing with the causes, diagnosis, treatment, and validity of milk allergy; however, it is generally accepted that milk allergy is a sensitivity to the protein in milk. These proteins are casein, lactalbumin, and lactoglobulins. Casein (also seen as sodium caseinate) accounts for about four-fifths of the protein in milk, while lactalbumins and lactoglobulins found in the whey of the milk constitute the remainder. Typically, people with a protein allergy to milk will react with the classic signs of allergy—eczema, rash, mucous buildup, wheezing, asthma. This buildup of mucous also occurs in the intestine, preventing the proper absorption of the carbohydrate (lactose) in milk, so diarrhea often develops.

In infants, this can be noticed as early as nine days, particularly if the parents have allergies themselves. Especially offensive is cow's milk, which contains over twice the amount of protein as human milk. An infant's system simply cannot always handle the digestion of these huge amounts of proteins, and they pass whole through the intestine to the bloodstream,

where they are treated as foreign properties by the body.
Allergic symptoms will ensue. In a nursing baby, the same thing
can happen when the mother drinks too much milk herself. The
offending protein passes through the breast milk and on to the
baby, often causing trouble.

## WHAT ARE THE SYMPTOMS
## OF MILK ALLERGY?

Generally, symptoms of milk allergy are similar to those of other
allergies, that is, respiratory in nature. Infants may have stuffiness, mucous in the stools, vomiting, and often a skin rash or
eczema. They will naturally be irritable and uncomfortable.
Allergists identify some typical clues for suspected milk allergy
among older babies and young children. It is not unusual to
notice dark blue, black, or red eye circles. These are called
"allergic shiners." Some children have reddish earlobes or a
glazed look in their eyes. Some do a constant push up on the
nose because it is itchy. This has been named "the allergic
salute." Adults generally better tolerate milk protein, but they
can also be sensitive and have these typical symptoms. Other
possible symptoms include bed wetting among young children,
lethargy or fatigue, inattentiveness. And while there is no hard
evidence for or against these signs as concrete symptoms for
milk protein allergy, their existence should be monitered.

# Making the Diagnosis

The whole subject of allergy is a tough one to tackle because the
truth is there isn't enough concrete information on which to
base a solid diagnosis or management plan. We do know that a
milk protein allergy means that people must stop using milk and
all other dairy products, because a continuous assault on the
system by protein allergens can cause real damage. Milk-allergic
infants must be protected from developing asthma or prolonged
diarrhea, which can cause dehydration.

# Allergy Tests

The problem with allergy tests is that no method has yet proved to be completely accurate and conclusive. Skin tests, often called "scratch tests," are not always reliable when many potential allergens are tested at once. Blood studies easily detect allergies to dust, mold, and pollen, but unfortunately, some people have been known to show no discernible blood reaction to foods, although their observed behavior after eating suggests that an allergy exists. Challenge tests in which suspected foods are withdrawn from the diet and then replaced systematically are reliable, though often impractical. Many people are allergic to several foods including milk and could assume that when milk is withdrawn from the diet during a challenge test and symptoms persist that milk is not the offender. But it is possible and quite likely that they may be reacting to another allergen too—one that has *not* been withdrawn from the diet, like wheat or corn or eggs.

Still, challenge tests can be implemented by either your physician or by you in an effort to pin down some food allergies. Suspicious foods, in this case milk and other dairy products, must be totally eliminated for about two weeks. Then add milk as a trial, perhaps one glass per meal. Do this for several days in a row, because sometimes allergic symptoms take time to manifest. If you react in an allergic manner, you can be reasonably sure that milk is the offender.

**Do Not Do Challenge Tests on Infants.** Their reactions could be sudden and life threatening. Instead, if you suspect your baby is allergic to the protein in milk, check with your physician about diagnosis and treatment. A widely accepted course of action is to have parents change their baby's formula from cow's milk to soy and watch for allergic symptoms to subside. Your child's pediatrician may also recommend a Stool Acidity Test, other stool cultures to test for offending bacterial infections, or a Sweat Chloride Test, which identifies cystic fibrosis. When the results of these tests are negative, a milk allergy is presumed.

# WHAT IS THE TREATMENT
# FOR MILK ALLERGY?

Infants who are allergic to milk protein will be placed on a soy-protein formula. About 25 percent of milk-allergic infants are sensitive to soy protein as well. The alternative then will be a pre-digested formula, which has all the proteins and carbo-hydrates hydrolyzed. As they grow, these babies might be able to handle small amounts of milk reasonably well. Otherwise they may continue to drink soy milks, which come in a variety of flavors. Unlike their lactose intolerant counterparts, children who are allergic to milk will not be able to have any fermented milk products like yogurt or aged cheese. But sometimes they will be able to have products made with whey, the part of milk that has more lactose than protein.

Later on, most children are able to tolerate some milk products without any allergic symptoms due to a more mature immune system. Based on current information, physicians do not believe that severe allergic reactions to milk protein last through adulthood.

Self-monitoring and self-management are very important when treating allergies. This is such a subjective issue, people responding differently under different circumstances, that aller-gists rely on personal observation to help guide allergy treat-ment. Each person has his own threshold for allergic responses and must be aware of his personal limitations. For example, if a ten-year-old girl has hay fever, the worst time for her would be late August through mid-October, the typical hay fever season. If she also has a milk protein allergy, this would not be a good time to experiment with dairy products because her allergic threshold is already being taxed. If she is also sensitive to eggs, her hay fever symptoms could be worse if she inadvertently eats something prepared with eggs. At other times of the year she might be able to have some baked goods prepared with both milk and eggs and not have much of an allergic reaction.

It is important to know that there are strong differences of opinion among physicians with relation to allergy treatment.

Some are proponents of dietary changes; others are not. Some have success with allergy extract therapy (shots), while others choose to handle allergies with drugs. Some like sub-lingual treatments, while others swear by nasal sprays. With allergy, no one's word is gospel, and what works for the Smiths down the block could be useless for you or your child. Your participation in your diagnosis and therapy is vital because one system cannot work for everyone. Allergies are subjective, and handling the problem for you or your child will require your being well informed, steadfast, and patient. New research is being done all the time that will hopefully yield important information for the benefit of those grappling with allergies of all kinds.

# 4

# The Question of Calcium

Calcium is a mineral we cannot do without. It provides our bones and teeth with their strength, and lies in reserve there until needed during periods of growth or pregnancy. It is essential for the clotting of our blood, the work of our cells, and the transmission of our nerve impulses. Without proper amounts of calcium in our bodies, our bones would be soft and easily fractured, our teeth would be in a state of constant decay, and our general health would be diminished. Calcium has proven to be a factor in high blood pressure, osteoporosis, periodontal bone loss, and colon cancer.

But calcium does not work alone. It must have other vitamins and minerals present to function. So worrying about calcium by itself is only facing part of the problem. Calcium works with phosphorus, potassium, sodium, magnesium, and vitamins A, C, and D. All of these must be present in our system for calcium absorption and utilization to take place.

Individual body need is another factor that affects calcium absorption. It seems that as we need more calcium, more is absorbed through our food. Healthy adults who eat a diet that meets minimum requirements for calcium absorb about 30 percent of the calcium from their food. Growing children and pregnant and nursing mothers absorb over 40 percent of the calcium in their food. People who overdo the amount of calcium they take in will absorb less. Conversely, people who customarily take in less calcium than normal will do a better job of absorbing it.

Getting enough calcium from your diet is easy if you can eat dairy products. If not, this most important source of calcium and vitamin D in the diet will have been eliminated. While there are other foods that provide calcium, dairy foods are by far the richest, most bountiful source. Giving up dairy foods does not mean that getting enough calcium is an impossibility. It just means that proper attention to the alternative food choices must be paid, and combining calcium-rich foods with your favorite foods needs to be done all day long, every day. Also, it is imperative that as much be done as possible to facilitate calcium absorption. That means getting your daily requirement of vitamins D, C, and A, and potassium, phosphorus, and magnesium. If you are unable or unwilling to take time to do this, then both vitamin and mineral supplementation is your next best alternative.

## SHOULD I TAKE SUPPLEMENTS OR GIVE THEM TO MY CHILDREN?

The best way to decide about taking supplements is to first know how much vitamins and minerals are required for you personally, then learn which foods contain the essential vitamins and minerals. If you will eat these foods each day, you probably will not require a calcium or vitamin supplement. If you cannot imagine yourself or your child eating the necessary foods, it would be wise to take supplements or give them to your child.

Locate yourself on Table 3, entitled RECOMMENDED DAILY DIETARY ALLOWANCES. This information is provided by the Food and Nutrition Board, National Academy of

Table 3

*Recommended Daily Dietary Allowances

| | Age | Vit. A | Vit. D | Vit. C | Calcium | Phosphorus | Magnesium |
|---|---|---|---|---|---|---|---|
| Infants | 0-6 mos. | 1400 IU | 400 IU | 35 mg | 360 mg | 240 mg | 50 mg |
| | 6-12 mos. | 1400 IU | 400 IU | 35 mg | 540 mg | 360 mg | 70 mg |
| Children | 1-3 | 1400 IU | 400 IU | 45 mg | 800 mg | 800 mg | 150 mg |
| | 4-6 | 2500 IU | 400 IU | 45 mg | 800 mg | 800 mg | 200 mg |
| | 7-10 | 3300 IU | 400 IU | 45 mg | 800 mg | 800 mg | 250 mg |
| Males | 11-14 | 5000 IU | 400 IU | 50 mg | 1200 mg | 1200 mg | 350 mg |
| | 15-18 | 5000 IU | 400 IU | 60 mg | 1200 mg | 1200 mg | 400 mg |
| | 19-22 | 5000 IU | 300 IU | 60 mg | 800 mg | 800 mg | 350 mg |
| | 23-50 | 5000 IU | 200 IU | 60 mg | 800 mg | 800 mg | 350 mg |
| | 51 + | 5000 IU | 200 IU | 60 mg | 800 mg | 800 mg | 350 mg |
| Females | 11-14 | 4000 IU | 400 IU | 50 mg | 1200 mg | 1200 mg | 300 mg |
| | 15-18 | 4000 IU | 400 IU | 60 mg | 1200 mg | 1200 mg | 300 mg |
| | 19-22 | 4000 IU | 300 IU | 60 mg | * 800 mg | 800 mg | 300 mg |
| | 23-50 | 4000 IU | 200 IU | 60 mg | * 800 mg | 800 mg | 300 mg |
| | 51 + | 4000 IU | 200 IU | 60 mg | * 800 mg | 800 mg | 300 mg |
| Pregnant | | 5000 IU | 600 IU | 80 mg | *1200 mg | 1200 mg | 450 mg |
| Lactating | | 6000 IU | 600 IU | 100 mg | *1200 mg | 1200 mg | 450 mg |

Food and Nutrition Board, National Academy of Sciences/ National Research Council. Updated 1980

* Other government sources indicate that adult women should have 1000 mg calcium per day. Pregnant women and women over 50 need 1500 mg per day.

Sciences, National Research Council. Write down your RDA for calcium, phosphorus, magnesium, potassium, and vitamins A, C, and D. Next, check the appropriate food sources and calculate how much of the food source alternatives you should be eating each day. If it sounds feasible for you, then you should get all your vitamin and mineral nutrients from your diet. If not, rely on supplementation.

The U.S. Department of Agriculture reports that a ten-year study of 35,000 Americans found that 68 percent of the population does not meet the recommended dietary allowances for calcium. Those who most need it, adolescent girls and middle-aged women, were generally very deficient in calcium. The study showed that girls between the ages of 15 and 18 were 87 percent calcium deficient. Women from 35 to 50 were 84 percent deficient.

|          |           | RDA Potassium | Sodium       |
|----------|-----------|---------------|--------------|
| Infants  | 0-6 mos.  | 350-925 mg    | 115-350 mg   |
|          | 6-12 mos. | 425-1275 mg   | 250-750 mg   |
| Children | 1-3       | 550-1650 mg   | 325-975 mg   |
|          | 4-6       | 775-2325 mg   | 450-1350 mg  |
|          | 7-10      | 1000-3000 mg  | 600-1800 mg  |
|          | 11 +      | 1525-4575 mg  | 900-2700 mg  |
| Adults   |           | 1875-5625 mg  | 1100-3300 mg |

### FOOD SOURCES OF RECOMMENDED
### VITAMINS AND MINERALS

*Calcium:*   Dairy products are the richest sources of calcium. Other sources include canned salmon with bones, clams, oysters, shrimp, mustard greens, turnip greens, kale, collard greens.

| FOOD SOURCE | AMOUNT | MG CALCIUM |
| --- | --- | --- |
| Yogurt, Plain | 1 cup | 415 |
| Yogurt, Fruited | 1 cup | 345 |
| Collard Greens | 1 cup | 289 |
| Milk | 1 cup | 288 |
| Swiss Cheese | 1 ounce | 272 |
| Dandelion Greens | 1 cup | 252 |
| Turnip Greens | 1 cup | 252 |
| Mackerel, Canned/Bones | 3 ounces | 263 |
| Sockeye Salmon/Bones | 3.5 ounces | 260 |
| Sardines in Oil | 8 medium | 260 |
| Soyamel Formula | 1 cup | 240 |
| Isomil Formula | 1 cup | 230 |
| Cheddar Cheese | 1 ounce | 204 |
| American Processed Cheese | 1 ounce | 198 |
| Mustard Greens | 1 cup | 193 |
| Tofu | ½ cup | 188 |
| Cooked Spinach | 1 cup | 167 |
| Oats, Instant Fortified | 1 packet | 164 |
| Oysters, Canned | 3.5 ounces | 152 |
| Kale | 1 cup | 147 |
| Beet Greens | 1 cup | 144 |
| Brussels Sprouts | 1 cup | 138 |
| Broccoli | 1 cup | 136 |
| Shrimp | 3.5 ounces | 115 |

*Phosphorus:*   Phosphorus works hand in hand with calcium for many functions, including healthy bone and tooth formation. Foods rich in calcium are also good sources of phosphorus.

| FOOD SOURCE | AMOUNT | MG PHOSPHORUS |
|---|---|---|
| Brewer's Yeast | 3.5 ounces (100 gms) | 1,753 |
| Brazil Nuts | 3.5 ounces | 694 |
| Walnuts | 3.5 ounces | 570 |
| Almonds | 3.5 ounces | 504 |
| Bran Flakes | 3.5 ounces | 495 |
| Sardines | 3.5 ounces | 478 |
| Peanut Butter | 3.5 ounces | 407 |
| Peanuts, Roasted | 3.5 ounces | 407 |
| Tuna, Canned | 3.5 ounces | 394 |
| Cashews, Unsalted | 3.5 ounces | 373 |
| Wheat Flakes Cereal | 3.5 ounces | 309 |
| Pecans | 3.5 ounces | 289 |
| Bluefish | 3.5 ounces | 287 |
| Chicken, w/o Skin | 3.5 ounces | 265 |
| Beef | 3.5 ounces | 246 |
| Lamb | 3.5 ounces | 223 |
| Popcorn | 3.5 ounces | 216 |
| Eggs, Whole | 3.5 ounces | 205 |
| Lobster | 3.5 ounces | 192 |
| Noodles, Enriched | 3.5 ounces | 183 |
| Beans, Cooked, White | 3.5 ounces | 148 |
| Beans, Cooked, Red | 3.5 ounces | 140 |

*Magnesium:*    Works for the health and formation of bones and teeth. Important for carbohydrate metabolism. Works to promote muscle and nerve action.

| FOOD SOURCE | AMOUNT | MG MAGNESIUM |
| --- | --- | --- |
| Cashew Nuts | 3.5 ounces (100 gms) | 373 |
| Almonds | 3.5 ounces | 270 |
| Brewer's Yeast | 3.5 ounces | 231 |
| Brazil Nuts | 3.5 ounces | 225 |
| Walnuts | 3.5 ounces | 190 |
| Peanuts | 3.5 ounces | 175 |
| Peanut Butter | 3.5 ounces | 173 |
| Beans, White | 3.5 ounces | 170 |
| Beans, Red | 3.5 ounces | 163 |
| Pecans | 3.5 ounces | 142 |
| Wheat Cereal, Shredded | 3.5 ounces | 133 |

*Potassium:*    Potassium is an essential component of all cells. It is responsible for the maintenance of proper fluid pressure and balance. It is also essential for energy and muscle function, including the heart.

| FOOD SOURCE | AMOUNT | MG POTASSIUM |
| --- | --- | --- |
| Brewer's Yeast | 3.5 ounces (100 gms) | 1894 |
| Beans, Red | 3.5 ounces | 984 |
| Apricots, Dried | 3.5 ounces | 979 |
| Wheat Germ | 3.5 ounces | 827 |
| Almonds | 3.5 ounces | 773 |
| Brazil Nuts | 3.5 ounces | 715 |
| Prunes, Dried | 3.5 ounces | 694 |

*(Continued on next page)*

| FOOD SOURCE | AMOUNT | MG POTASSIUM |
|---|---|---|
| Peanuts | 3.5 ounces | 674 |
| Dates | 3.5 ounces | 648 |
| Figs, Dried | 3.5 ounces | 640 |
| Avocado | 3.5 ounces | 604 |
| Pecans | 3.5 ounces | 603 |
| Veal | 3.5 ounces | 500 |
| Scallops, Bay | 3.5 ounces | 476 |
| Cashew Nuts | 3.5 ounces | 464 |
| Calves Liver | 3.5 ounces | 453 |
| Banana | 1 | 440 |
| Beans, Lima | 3.5 ounces | 422 |
| Chicken | 3.5 ounces | 411 |
| Beef | 3.5 ounces | 370 |

*Vitamin A and Carotene:*   There are several essential functions of vitamin A in the body, and most deal with the health of mucous membranes, including the intestine. It is an important vitamin necessary for maintaining normal vision, healthy skin, and proper absorption. Large amounts of vitamin A can be toxic. Carotene is the yellow pigment in plants that is converted into a vitamin A substance in the body. Large amounts of carotene are not toxic, although the skin could show an orangish tinge.

| FOOD SOURCE | AMOUNT | IU VITAMIN A |
|---|---|---|
| Carrots, Cooked | 1 cup | 15,220 |
| Pumpkin, Canned | 1 cup | 14,590 |
| Spinach, Canned | 1 cup | 14,580 |
| Sweet Potatoes | 1 cup | 13,000 |
| Collards, Cooked | 1 cup | 10,260 |
| Kale | 1 cup | 8140 |

| FOOD SOURCE | AMOUNT | IU VITAMIN A |
| --- | --- | --- |
| Beet Greens | 1 cup | 7400 |
| Cantaloupe | ½ melon | 6540 |
| Carrots, Raw | 1 whole | 5500 |
| Broccoli | 1 cup | 3880 |
| Dried Apricots | 3 whole | 2890 |
| Vegetable Soup | 1 cup | 2500 |
| Endive | 2 ounces | 1870 |
| Swordfish | 3 ounces | 1750 |
| Peach | 1 whole | 1320 |
| Asparagus | 1 cup | 1310 |
| Tomato Soup | 1 cup | 1200 |
| Green Beans | 1 cup | 680 |
| Egg | 1 whole | 590 |
| Lima Beans | 1 cup | 480 |

*Vitamin D:* This is the vitamin essential for calcium absorption. It is necessary to prevent rickets, a deficiency disease that causes stunted growth and deformed bones. It was added to milk for that general purpose. Vitamin D is not found readily in foods but is manufactured in the body as a result of exposure to sunlight. If you live in a sunny area and spend time outdoors each day, you may not need to supplement your diet with vitamin D. Large amounts of this vitamin are toxic, so be careful not to over-compensate.

| FOOD SOURCE | AMOUNT | IU VITAMIN D |
| --- | --- | --- |
| Cod Liver Oil | ⅛ ounce | 500 |
| Halibut Liver Oil | one capsule | 400 |
| Cod Liver Oil | one capsule | 200 |

*Vitamin C:*   Vitamin C is ascorbic acid. Its principal function is to work with collagen, properly forming out bones, teeth, and blood vessels. It is a constituent of wound healing and has the ability to help us fight infection. It is neither produced by the body nor stored there. It must be replaced every day.

| FOOD SOURCE | AMOUNT | MG VITAMIN C |
|---|---|---|
| Broccoli | 1 cup | 143 |
| Orange Juice | 1 cup | 100 |
| Grapefruit Juice | 1 cup | 92 |
| Strawberries | 1 cup | 88 |
| Orange | 1 fruit | 66 |
| Cantaloupe | ½ melon | 63 |
| Grapefruit | ½ fruit | 44 |

## TABLE 4

### GETTING THE MOST OUT OF YOUR CALCIUM SOURCE

#### WAYS TO AID CALCIUM ABSORPTION

1.  Make sure to have the required daily allowance of vitamin D, vitamin C, vitamin A or carotene, phosphorus, magnesium, and potassium.
2.  Maintain normal motility of the digestive system.
3.  Exercise by walking, biking, or working out gently with weights if you are at risk for osteoporosis.
4.  If you take supplement pills, be sure you take them with plenty of water to help the breakdown.

#### THE FOLLOWING BLOCK THE ABSORPTION OF CALCIUM:

1.  Alcohol
2.  Smoking

3. High Fat Foods

4. Sodium

5. Stress

6. Lack of Exercise

7. Caffeine

8. Oxalic Acid: found in spinach, swiss chard, beet tops, cocoa, and rhubarb. Do not use these foods as an important calcium source.

9. Phytic Acid: found in the outer layers of cereal grains. This is important if the diet is composed of whole grain cereals as a major component.

## TABLE 5

### FOOD SOURCE CHART

#### YOUR DAILY NEEDS

| | |
|---|---|
| Calcium | _____ mg |
| Phosphorus | _____ mg |
| Magnesium | _____ mg |
| Potassium | _____ mg |
| Vitamin A | _____ IU |
| Vitamin D | _____ IU |
| Vitamin C | _____ mg |

#### FOODS TO BE INCLUDED IN MY DAILY DIET

Calcium Foods:                          Serving Size:

_____

_____

_____

_____

Phosphorus Foods:                   Serving Size:

_____

_____

_____

_____


Magnesium Foods:                    Serving Size:

_____

_____

_____

_____


Potassium Foods:                    Serving Size:

_____

_____

_____

_____


Vitamin A Foods:                    Serving Size:

_____

_____

_____

_____


Vitamin D Foods:                    Serving Size:

_____

_____

_____

_____

Vitamin C Foods:                    Serving Size:

_____

_____

_____

_____

_____

_____

_____

_____

_____

_____

# Choosing a Calcium Supplement

If, after filling out your Food Source Chart, you decide that you should take supplements, choosing the necessary ones will be the next step. You will want to choose vitamin and mineral supplements that are complete, well absorbed, and cost efficient. *Do not take more than your requirements.* You certainly don't need complications caused by vitamin and mineral toxicity. Most likely you will take two supplements per day—a regular over-the-counter daily vitamin tablet and a calcium tablet. Make sure you are not double-dosing your vitamin D. *Do not choose a vitamin tablet with D and a calcium tablet with D.* That could be dangerous in the long run.

Calcium is available in several forms: gluconate, lactate, carbonate, and citrate. All of these are fine. *Do not* take dolomite or bone meal as they have been linked with lead poisoning. For calcium, one of the most essential things to consider is how quickly the tablets dissolve. A study done at the University of Maryland School of Pharmacy in 1987 reports that out of 35 calcium carbonate supplements, only 17 dissolved within the USP standard of 30 minutes. Fourteen disintegrated within 10 minutes or less, a very efficient time.

## TABLE 6

### THE SOLUBILITY OF CALCIUM SUPPLEMENTS

*The Best*   These have a high rate of dissolution within 30 minutes.

| PRODUCT | MANUFACTURER | % DISSOLVED IN 30 MINUTES |
|---|---|---|
| Tums | Norcliff-Thayer | 100 |
| Calcium Carbonate | Roxane Labs | 100 |
| Oyster Shell Calcium with Vitamin D | Nature Made | 99 |
| Supplical | Warner Lambert | 98 |
| Calcimax | Norcliff-Thayer | 91 |
| Oscal 500 | Marion Lab | 87 |
| Calcium 600 with Vitamin D | Giant Food | 87 |
| Calcium 600 | Giant Food | 80 |
| Caltrate 600 | Lederle Laboratories | 69 |
| Natural Calcium 600 | Foods Plus | 66 |

*The Worst*   None of these dissolved to a measurable degree within 30 minutes.

| PRODUCT | MANUFACTURER |
|---|---|
| Calcium 600-D | AARP Pharmacy |
| Calcium 600 | Gray Drug Fair |
| Natural Oyster Shell | Gray Drug Fair |
| Sea-Cal | Natural Sales |
| Calcium 600D | Plus Products Pathmark |

*To Test Your Brand of Calcium Supplements at Home:*   Drop one tablet in a glass of vinegar. If it hasn't dissolved after 30 minutes, it isn't absorbing fast enough. Or, put your tablet in a clear glass (breaking it into bits if it is a chewable), cover with ¼ cup hot water, and shake it up periodically during an hour. If it dissolves in 24 hours or less, it is acceptable.

**Table 7**

THE COST OF COMPARING CALCIUM SUPPLEMENTS

| PRODUCT—MG PER | # OF TABLETS DAILY | COST PER DAY |
|---|---|---|
| Calcet/153 g | 6-10 | 43¢ |
| Calcicaps/125 mg | 7-10 | 21¢ |
| Calcitrel/200 mg | 4-5 | 15¢ |
| Cal-Sup 300/300 mg | 3-5 | 20¢ |
| Cal-Sup 600 with Vitamin D/600 mg | 2 | 20¢ |
| Cal-Sup 600 Plus Vitamin C & D/600 mg | 2 | 20¢ |
| Caltrate 600/600 mg | 2 | 24¢ |
| Caltrate 600 + D/600 mg | 2 | 24¢ |
| Caltrate Jr. Chewable 300 mg | 3 | 25¢ |
| Citracal/200 mg | 8-10 | 56¢ |
| Generic Oyster Shell Calcium/500 mg | 2 | 6¢ |
| Nature Made 100% Oyster Shell Calcium/250 mg | 4 | 12¢ |
| Os-Cal 500/500 mg | 2 | 30¢ |
| Os-Cal 500D/500 mg | 2 | 30¢ |
| Os-Cal 500 Chewable 500 mg | 2 | 22¢ |
| Pac Man Chewable Calcium for Kids/300 mg | 3 | 36¢ |
| Suplical Vanilla Flavored Chewables/600 mg | 2 | 40¢ |
| Tums/200 mg each | 4-5 | 12¢ |
| Tums EX/300 mg | 3-4 | 15¢ |
| Your Life Calcium Hi-Cal/500 mg | 2 | 4¢ |

# 5

# Milk and Kids—
# Not Always
# the Best Combination

Contrary to popular belief, milk and kids is not always the best combination. This was especially evident during the 1930s, 40s, and 50s when breastfeeding waned in popularity in America. Slowly, we saw the number of babies with allergic reactions grow, and parents had to deal with infant diarrhea, rashes, and wheezing. Scientists agree that cow's milk is the number one allergen in an infant's life and have proven that lactose intolerance is highly prevalent among babies and young children over the age of three. Studies have been done that measure the amount of antibodies in the bloodstream of infants that are breastfed compared to those that are fed cow's milk formula, and the results dramatically highlight the inappropriateness of cow's milk in the infant diet.

While lactose intolerance may be an inherited trait, it can also be secondary to milk protein allergy. Scientists have observed mucosal lesions in the digestive system of babies who were being fed cow's milk protein. The continuous onslaught of the offending protein causes inflammation and the release of inflammatory mediators, which hamper absorption and damage the intestinal lining. In other words, a milk protein allergy that is not treated could bring about lactose intolerance.

Milk protein allergy is generally evident during the first three months of life. Symptoms are the classic signs of allergy: eczema, rash, wheezing, and stuffy, itchy nose. Once established, the infant may be colicky, may vomit quite a bit, and may have bloody diarrhea or considerable mucous in the stool.

While a proper diagnosis is important, it is sometimes difficult to differentiate between milk protein allergy and lactose intolerance, since the infant who is lactose intolerant will also have diarrhea and be uncomfortable, gassy, and irritable. It is possible, however, for your pediatrician to do a Stool Acidity Test. A fresh stool sample can be checked for acidity and for the presence of glucose. When lactose is not properly broken down in the intestine, it moves into the colon where bacteria convert it to lactic acid; thus, the acidity in the stool increases. Also, when small amounts of lactose are hydrolyzed in the colon and cannot be absorbed there, glucose is measurable in the colon. If the pediatrician finds a positive Stool Acidity Test, the infant is most likely lactose intolerant. If the results of this test are negative, a milk protein allergy is highly probable. Challenge tests, where infants are given cow's milk for a specified period of time and then have it withdrawn for a while and later reintroduced, are considered unwise for babies and young children. Serious allergic reactions could occur that present a real danger to the life of the baby.

For older children, some pediatricians recommend standard allergy tests, although the results of these are not uniformly reliable. In this case, a challenge test may be appropriate, but often not necessary, especially if eliminating milk and other dairy products from the diet produces positive results. That's usually evidence enough. Milk protein allergic children often have a bit of a reprieve from symptoms between the ages of one and five. Lactose intolerant children will usually become worse after age three. Observing your child's reactions to milk and reporting them to the pediatrician will have a strong impact on the diagnosis. In either case, treatment is still the same: **eliminate the milk.**

The first step in treatment for the milk-sensitive infant is a switch to a soy protein formula such as Isomil, Nursoy, or Prosobee. These formulas are readily available and comparable in cost to other standard formulas. Twenty-five percent of these infants are allergic to soy protein as well as cow's milk protein. For them, a substitution may be made with formulas that have their protein pre-hydrolyzed (predigested). These would be Nutramigen or Pregestimil. These two are often given to premature infants whose digestive systems are highly sensitive due to their immaturity. For the breastfed infant, mother must be sure to eliminate milk and dairy products from *her* diet, but she should be sure to maintain proper calcium levels with a supplement. Some infants do best when a combination of breast milk and soy formula is worked out.

Recently, the use of lactase enzymes has been introduced into the infant diet. Expressed breast milk can be treated with the enzyme to reduce the lactose content. Lactase enzyme drops have also been tried for breastfeeding infants by putting the drops directly on the mother's nipple so the baby ingests the enzyme during nursing. This is extremely helpful for milk-protein-allergic infants who will benefit from the protective antibody properties of breast milk.

Milk-free formulas can be used for a long time after infancy. Toddlers can continue to drink these formulas with meals, yet parents may wish to dilute the formula more than usual to cut back on the calories for the older baby. Later, small children may drink soy milks that are available in health food stores. They come in a variety of flavors including chocolate and strawberry. Some of these flavored soy milks come in aseptic packages that need no refrigeration until opening, perfect for a school lunchbox.

As the young child grows, it is possible to confirm a lactose intolerant condition through a breath hydrogen test. Children are given 1-2 grams of lactose per kilogram of their body

weight. The lactose is mixed in lemonade and their breath
hydrogen is measured before drinking the lactose load. Afterward, their breath hydrogen measurement is taken periodically.
A blood glucose test may be done in this manner also. For
children with a confirmed lactose intolerance, it will be important for their parents to be aware of exactly how much milk, if
any, their child can tolerate. Likewise, yogurt and aged cheeses
should be tried because these will add a very important calcium
source. Milk-protein-allergic children should also be challenged
periodically as their digestive system matures. This type of
protein allergy does not usually extend through adulthood.

## WHAT ABOUT CALCIUM
## SUPPLEMENTS FOR CHILDREN?

This is an area that has not had wide support from pediatricians,
although the pendulum seems to be shifting of late. Remember
that children who are on milk-free diets will usually better
absorb the calcium from other foods. If your child will accept
other calcium sources like salmon with bones, tofu, sardines,
broccoli, collard greens, or kale, supplementation may not be
necessary. If these food cannot be part of your child's *everyday
diet,* then supplementation is advisable. Many parents also
choose to give their children a daily vitamin supplement during
periods of non-eating or if their child is particularly fussy. Proper
vitamin levels are necessary for calcium absorption. A hot dog
and peanut butter-and-jelly diet just won't do it. In response to
this need, several children's vitamin manufacturers have begun
to add essential minerals to their chewables. The following
children's vitamin supplements provide some calcium:

> Bugs Bunny Sugarfree + Minerals, 100 mg.
> Centrum Jr. + C, 108 mg calcium (*contains lactose*)
> Centrum Jr. + Calcium, 160 mg calcium (*contains lactose*)
> Centrum Jr. + Iron, 108 mg calcium (*contains lactose*)
> Sunkist Chewables, 100 mg calcium
> ViPenta Drops, 100 mg calcium

There are also chewable calcium tablets on the market:

Caltrate Jr., 300 mg calcium per tablet (orange flavored)
Os-Cal Chewable, 500 mg calcium per tablet (Bavarian creme flavored)
Suplical, 600 mg calcium per tablet (vanilla flavored)

## HELPING YOUR BABY FEEL BETTER

If your baby has had diarrhea for a long time or has been vomiting several times a day, there are some things you can do to help her feel better soon. The most important, of course, is eliminating the offending cow's milk. Pay attention to her stools and notice whether there is any blood or mucous present. Report this to your doctor right away. He may wish to prescribe some calming medication. Dilute the new milk-free formula for the first week or so and gradually build up to full strength. Increased amounts of water are necessary for digestive distress recovery. Offer your baby lots of water in between feedings to help with rehydration and stool formation. *Do not feed your baby solid foods.* If she was eating cereal or fruit, stop these altogether since they may not be tolerated well now. The digestive system needs time to recover from a bout of diarrhea, and solid foods only tax the system more. More frequent bottle feedings may be necessary, and don't hold back because of a schedule. This transition time may last up to six weeks, and the schedule can wait to be established. Your baby's needs are much too important now to be worried about the clock. Once she feels better, everything will fall into place.

After the stools return to normal, consider feeding solids again, but check with your pediatrician first. Chances are if your baby is less than four or five months old, you needn't bother. Babies usually cannot digest solids until after that time anyway, and the notion that solids help them sleep is just a myth. They will sleep well when their digestive system is healthy and relaxed.

Love is especially important. And there is even scientific evidence to prove love's healing and growing power. While your baby is uncomfortable, she will need more rocking, stroking, massaging, and holding than usual. Don't worry about "spoiling" her. Remember that she is in pain and needs your love and affection to help her feel better and thrive. When the pain subsides, and this may take a week or more, she should be happier, more relaxed, and content. Mothers have known for ages that extra loving can do a lot for a baby. For many children with digestive distress, love is their most important nourishment for a while. Babies with food sensitivities often keep very little of the food down at all. And yet, with proper care, they will continue to gain weight and thrive.

Some babies are more comfortable on your shoulder, with their knees bent and your hand supporting their feet. Some babies are most comfortable in a small crib wrapped up tightly in a blanket. For severe abdominal pain, parents can make a baby "heating pad" consisting of a *warm*, not hot, water bottle wrapped in a cloth diaper or receiving blanket. Place this baby "heating pad" on your lap and lay the baby across with her tummy on the heated area and her head gently cradled in your hands. Slowly rock her from side to side. A soothing voice or song doesn't hurt either. Some infants respond to relaxation tapes of ocean waters or rippling lake water. The key is to find what works for your child and stick with it. Making her as comfortable as possible is really important, and she will reward you in ways that only babies can.

# HELPING YOUR CHILD RECOVER FROM A TUMMY UPSET

If your child has just learned about his milk allergy or lactose intolerance, you may be unsure about the best way to feed him during or after a bout of diarrhea. Check with your physician on this, because sometimes doctors do prescribe medication.

The following is a recommended procedure for feeding during these times:

1. Eliminate solid foods from the diet.
2. Put your child on a liquid diet to replace essential fluids and lost minerals, the lack of which contribute to the lethargy that accompanies diarrhea. Include these: broth, water, gelatin, diluted fruit or vegetable juice, soft drinks, bouillon, weak tea, and decaffeinated coffee.
3. Be sure to include orange juice and beef broth as part of the liquid diet. Both are rich in the potassium needed to make your child feel stronger.
4. Continue this regimen for at least twenty-four hours or until a stool begins to form.
5. Slowly add solid foods, beginning with breads and cereals, rice, potatoes, or eggs that are boiled or poached.
6. Steamed vegetables and light meats may be added next.
7. Slowly work your way up to raw fruits and vegetables, being sure to include carrots, which are rich in beta carotene and vital for digestive health.
8. Next, add red meats and dishes comprised of a combination of foods.

Don't tax the digestive system when your child has diarrhea since it needs time to recuperate. He may eventually be able to recover quite quickly from an episode, perhaps within twenty-four hours. Later, you may wish to experiment with small amounts of dairy products to find his healthy tolerance level. Remember to eliminate all forms of lactose or milk protein during a bout with diarrhea. The diarrhea itself will cause enzyme depletion that will only add fuel to the fire. A heating pad or hot water bottle may offer some comfort. Your child will need to rest some but probably won't need to have many activities restricted.

If he's really hungry during the first twenty-four hours, consider it a good sign, but don't overdo it. Offer him crackers with some light jelly or peanut butter spread on top, or fill his soup with rice or noodles. Milk-free homemade ice creams and popsicles will be a welcome treat.

## HELPING YOUR LITTLE ONES COPE

Life can be pretty hard on toddlers and small children sometimes. They have so many negatives in their lives already—so
much they'd love to get into but can't. Stringently restricting
their diet may add another negative dimension, and yet it has to
be done. So approach the whole process with gentleness and
flexibility. Now is not the time to enforce strict and unbendable
rules at the dinner table. Help your child feel comfortable about
his food choices. Teach him how food is prepared and let him be
part of the cooking fun. Being able to recognize which foods are
acceptable will help him to turn down offers of unacceptable
snacks and treats when he ventures out to school or a friend's
home.

There are many milk-free treats the whole family can enjoy:
popcorn, nuts and raisins, frozen juice pops, gelatin desserts,
milk-free ice creams, and baked goods. Giving up store-bought
snacks may seem tough at first, but think how much more
healthful they will be when you prepare them at home, and
allowing your child to help with the cooking will provide some
old-fashioned family fun. Many parents who are busy at work
all week make up several milk-free dishes and treats for the
freezer on Saturdays or Sundays.

Kids love to pack a lunchbox or goody bag. Chances are your
child will have many opportunities to do just that, because he
may have to bring his own snacks to day care or a neighbor's
home. Personalized bags are always fun to make and receive.
They will help your child feel that his food is "special," and
taking it along will be fun, not bothersome. At school, be sure
to let the teacher know that your child can't have milk during
lunch or snack time. If the school's lunch program does not
offer a juice alternative, you may have to provide your own
juice. Some school systems are quite open to suggestions and
may choose to offer a juice alternative when informed about the
prevalence of lactose intolerance and milk allergy among children. It's worth a try. As more parents of milk-sensitive children

speak out, we will see more changes made in the lunchrooms across the country. Have a talk with your child's school or day-care provider.

## RECURRENT ABDOMINAL PAIN (RAP)

Physicians are often faced with children who have stomach or abdominal pain. Diagnosing the problem can be tricky. A syndrome called Recurrent Abdominal Pain, or RAP, was described in the early 1960s and is defined by the presence of several episodes of pain, severe enough to affect a child's activities, happening at least once a month for three months in a row. The incidence of RAP is thought to be between 9-15 percent in the general pediatric population. Stress among children has been proven a factor in RAP, and peptic ulcer or urinary tract infection has also been identified among some of these children, though rarely. These children were generally very colicky babies. Children with RAP may be pale, constipated, or suffering from headaches as well. Some of these children grow up and develop inflammatory bowel disease, but most do not.

Studies performed on children with RAP have disclosed that approximately *40 percent of them were lactose intolerant.* These studies have also shown that physicians should not rely on the presence of diarrhea, the amount of milk normally consumed in a day, or the pain frequency when trying to identify lactose intolerance. A hydrogen breath test, however, is an important diagnostic tool.

The importance of these studies on RAP should have a great bearing on the way children with abdominal pain are treated by their physicians and in their homes. Recurrent Abdominal Pain should not automatically be assumed to be psychogenic if organic disease is not found. The fact is that 40 percent of the children who have these symptoms are lactose intolerant and require dietary management. Experts agree that invasive testing should be secondary to a dietary change that eliminates milk. A trial of lactose elimination followed by a period of putting the child back on his normal diet to see if the pain recurs is an important diagnostic procedure. If your child suffers from Recurrent Abdominal Pain and is not helped by a milk-free diet over a period of six to eight weeks, you should speak to his pediatrician. If further testing is required, you may want to consult with a pediatric gastroenterologist, a specialist in children's digestive disease.

Whatever you do, don't ever chastize your child for feeling sick. His pain is probably derived from a physical cause. If not, and your child's pain is a result of psychological or environmental stress, he must be treated by a proper professional. Helping your child get well, no matter what the cause of illness, is firm proof of your love and devotion. Your support will mean a great deal to your child now and in the future.

# 6

# Managing in the Store

## IN THE STORE

There are many federal regulations governing the information on a food label. Ingredients listed on food labels are in descending order of predominance; in other words, the first ingredient listed comprises the largest amount of the product, while the last ingredient listed comprises the least. Percentages are not always given and are not required to be on the label. Some labels are more informative than others because the manufacturer has voluntarily decided to disclose more information than required. That helps those of us who are looking out for particular ingredients. And no matter how large, companies do like to hear from the consumer when they are doing something right. Certain products can use optional ingredients that are not required to appear on the label, and lactose may be one of those that is not listed in foods. For example, the label might say "sugar" without being specific about which sugar was used.

None of these foods are legally required to have full content labeling:

canned fruit and juice
canned vegetables
cocoa products

enriched bread and rolls
flour
food flavorings
fruit butters, jellies, and preserves
fruit pies
frozen desserts
milk and cream products
natural cheeses and processed cheeses
nonalcoholic beverages
noodle products
raisin bread and rolls
salad dressing
white bread and rolls
whole wheat bread and rolls

When reading labels, check for and avoid all ingredients listed as milk in any form. Avoid all items with lactose and all items with whey, casein, sodium caseinate, lactalbumin, and lactoglobulin. *If you are lactose intolerant, you may be able to have milk protein.* But many people report symptoms from all milk products or by-products. Some people must avoid beef itself!

*Look for and avoid:*

Casein (milk protein)
Lactalbumin (milk protein)
Lactoglobulin (milk protein)
Lactose (milk sugar)
Sodium Caseinate (milk protein)
Whey (contains both milk sugar and milk protein)
Acidophilus milk
Buttermilk
Condensed milk
Cultured milk
Dried milk
Evaporated milk
Malted milk
Milk solids

Powdered milk
Skim milk
Whole milk

*Note:* Percentages on milk cartons refer to fat content only and have nothing to do with milk sugar or milk protein.

2% Milk = 2% Fat = Lowfat Milk
1% Milk = 1% Fat = Very Lowfat Milk
½ % Milk = ½% Fat = Skim Milk

The good news is that besides food items that are normally milk free, manufacturers have been able to produce many different and exciting items to market for the lactose-free, milk-protein-free needs of the consumer. Admittedly, if you live in a large metropolitan area, your choices will be better than those of us who live in small towns. But there are several companies who make milk-free foods that can be shipped through the mail. A complete list is at the end of this chapter. Write to these companies for more information.

It is important to remember that food manufacturers change their product ingredients because of price or availability. Therefore, it is necessary to always check labels frequently. Also, kosher dietary laws require that all foods containing no dairy products whatsoever are to be labeled *pareve.* Therefore, all items marked *pareve* are safe to eat. The Union of Orthodox Jewish Congregations of America marks all kosher food items with a ''U'' in a circle. If the symbol has a ''D'' after it, it means some sort of dairy product is being used in the food even though it may not be listed on the label.

Many foods can be pre-treated with a lactase enzyme. This will reduce the lactose content by about 70 percent. Some people can tolerate lactose at this level. Also, lactase enzyme tablets can be eaten just prior to having dairy foods, and that will also reduce the lactose content. Complete information on lactase enzyme products is in chapter seven. Many manufacturers have brought pre-treated items to the marketplace including lactose-reduced milk, cottage cheese, ice creams, and cheeses. If you cannot find any of these products in your store, feel free to write to the manufacturer. Find the address at the back of this chapter.

Here is a sample of some dairy-free foods available in your supermarket. Personally, I use very few prepared foods, so I cannot vouch for their quality.

These supermarket items are milk free:

*Appetizers*

Chinese Egg Rolls
Empire Kosher Meats and Chicken Party Packs
Ma Cohen's Kosher Products—Miniature Hot Dogs
and Turkey Franks

*Breads*

All authentic ethnic bread including: French, Italian, Challa,
Pits, Rye, Pumpernickel, Bagels
Kineret Kosher Frozen Challa Dough
Melba Toast—Plain and Garlic
Pepperidge Farm Club Rolls
Pepperidge Farm Patty Shells
Plain Ry-Krisp
Stella D'Oro Plain Breadsticks

*Pancakes and Mixes*

Aunt Jemima Buckwheat Pancake and Waffle Mix
Aunt Jemima Original Pancake and Waffle Mix
Aunt Jemima Whole Wheat Pancake and Waffle Mix
Hungry Jack Blueberry Pancake Mix
Hungry Jack Light Pancake Mix

*Crackers*

Honey Maid Graham Crackers
Keebler Crackers
Keebler Town House Oval Crackers
Nabisco Graham Crackers
Nabisco Premium Saltine Crackers

Nutty Wheat Thins Snack Crackers
Oysterettes Soup & Oyster Crackers
Potato 'n Sesame Snack Thins
Ritz Crackers
Sociables Crackers
Triscuit Whole Wheat Wafers
Uneeda Biscuit
Waverly Wafers
Wheatsworth Stone Ground Wheat Crackers
Zesta Saltine Crackers

*Milk-Free Meal Ideas*

Armour Classic Lites: Sliced Beef with Broccoli, Beef
  Pepper Steak, Veal Pepper Steak
Armour Dinner Classics: Beef Burgundy, Teriyaki Steak,
  Stuffed Green Peppers, Sweet & Sour Pork, Cod
  Almondine, Boneless Short Ribs with BBQ Sauce,
  Chicken Teriyaki, Sweet & Sour Chicken
Carnation Sandwich Spreads: Tuna Salad, Turkey Salad,
  Chicken Salad, Ham Salad
Chun King Foods: Beef Chow Mein, Chicken Chow
  Mein, Pork Chow Mein, Shrimp Chow Mein, Beef
  Pepper Oriental, Stir-Fry Vegetables and Sauce Mix, Boil-
  in-Bag-Chicken Chow Mein, Beef Pepper Oriental,
  Shrimp Chow Mein, Sweet and Sour Pork, Fried Rice
  with Pork
Hormel Canned Products: Spam, Deviled Ham, Ham
  Patties, Beans and Bacon, Pork Chow Mein, Sloppy Joes,
  Dinty Moore Corned Beef, Dinty Moore Beef Stew,
  Dinty Moore Hashed Potatoes and Beef
LaChoy Foods: Meat & Shrimp Egg Rolls, Chicken Egg
  Rolls, Shrimp Egg Rolls, Lobster Egg Rolls, Shrimp
  Chow Mein Dinner, Chicken Chow Mein Dinner, Beef
  Pepper Oriental Dinner, Sweet & Sour Pork, Sweet &
  Sour Chicken, Fried Rice with Meat, Chicken Won Ton
  Soup, Chicken Chow Mein, Shrimp Chow Mein
Lean Cuisine Dinner Supreme: Baked Chicken Breast,
  Beef Teriyaki

Lean Cuisine Entrees: Chicken a l'Orange with Almond
Rice, Chicken Cacciatore with Vermicelli, Chicken
Chow Mein with Rice, Linguini with Clam Sauce,
Meatball Stew, Oriental Beef with Vegetables and Rice,
Oriental Scallops and Vegetables with Rice, Stuffed
Cabbage with Meat in Tomato Sauce
Pillsbury Boil-in-Bag Entrees: Szechwan Beef, Chicken
with Garden Vegetables, Shrimp Creole
Signature Salads: Crabmeat Flavored Salad, Shrimp Salad,
Chicken Salad, Tuna Salad, Ham Salad, Egg Salad, Fresh
Button Mushroom Salad, Marinated Artichoke Salad,
Mexican Shrimp Salad Veracruz, Red Potato & Egg Salad
Supreme, Oriental Chicken Salad, Seafood Salad with
Crab & Shrimp, California Medley Salad, Garden Olive
Salad, Diced Potato Salad, Mustard Potato Salad, German
Potato Salad, Potato and Egg Salad, Macaroni Salad, Tri-
Bean Salad, Cucumber Salad, Carrot-Raisin Salad,
Gelatin Salads
Swanson Products: Chicken Nibbles with French Fries,
Fish 'n Chips, Salisbury Steak with Gravy, Breast
Portions, Fried Chicken, Nibbles, Thighs & Drumsticks,
Take-Out-Style Fried Chicken

*Meats*

Armour Meats (there may be a few exceptions)
Deviled Spam Luncheon Meat
Dinty Moore Beef Stew
Dinty Moore Corned Beef
Dinty Moore Hashed Potatoes and Beef
Empire Frozen Meats and Dinners
Feinberg Kosher Meats
Hebrew National Meats
Hormel Deviled Ham
Hormel Lunch Meats
Hormel Sausage (there may be a few exceptions)
Hormel Sloppy Joes
Louis Rich Turkey Products
Ma Cohen's Frozen Dinners

*Cereals*

Chex Cereals by Ralston Purina
Cream of Rice
Cream of Wheat
Nabisco Shredded Wheat
Nabisco 100% Bran Cereal
Quaker Cereals (there may be a few exceptions)
Quaker Instant Grits
Quaker Puffed Rice
Quaker Puffed Wheat
Quaker Quick Oats
Spoon-Size Shredded Wheat
Team Flakes

*Soups*

Check labels, but the following companies all make milk-
free soup:
Campbell's
Crosse & Blackwell
Goodman's
Great American
Knorr Swiss
Lipton
Pepperidge Farm
Tabachnik
Telma

*Beverages*

Country Time Drink Mixes
Country Time Sugar-Free Drink Mixes
Country Time Non-Carbonated Lemonade Flavor Drink
Crystal Light Sugar-Free Drink Mixes
Hawaiian Punch Flavor Crystals and Concentrates
Kool-Aid Koolers Juice Drinks
Kool-Aid Sugar-Sweetened Soft Drink Mixes

Kool-Aid Unsweetened Soft Drink Mixes
Tang Breakfast Beverage Crystals
Tang Sugar-Free Breakfast Beverage Crystals

*Pie Crust*

Apollo Phyllo Dough
Athena Phyllo Dough
Flako Pie Crust Mix
Johnston's Chocolate-Flavored Ready-Crust
Johnston's Graham Cracker Pie Crust
Oronoque Orchards Frozen Pie Crust

*Cake Mixes*

Duncan Hines: Devil's Food, Marble, Yellow, Lemon,
    Angel Food, Sponge Cake
Manischewitz Chocolate Chiffon
Pillsbury Chocolate Macaroon Bundt Cake Mix
Pillsbury Fudge and Walnut Brownie Mixes
Pillsbury Gingerbread Mix
Pillsbury Plus Cake Mixes—All flavors *except* Strawberry,
    Carrot 'n Spice, White, and Butter Recipe

*Desserts*

Baskin-Robbins Sorbets and Ices
Dole Fruit Sorbet
Gourmet Tofu by Riviera
Ice Bean
Jello Gelatin Pops
Le Sorbet by Haagen Daz
McGreen's Natural Dairy-Free Frozen Dessert
Mocha Mix
Parvelle
Penguino's
Popsicles
Rice Dream
Ta Tou Lite by Phoenix Foods
Tofair

Tofutti: Wildberry, Vanilla Almond, Chocolate, Peanut
   Butter, Love Drops, Tofutti Cuties
Tofulicious
Tuscan Dairy Farms Tofu Bars

*Milk Substitutes*

Eden Foods Soymilks (Plain, Vanilla, Chocolate,
   Strawberry)
Lactaid Specially Digestible Lactose-Reduced Milk
   (70% lactose-reduced)
Mocha Mix
Perx Frozen Non-Dairy Milk Substitute
Rich's Coffeerich (cholesterol free)
Rich's Polyrich (cholesterol free)
Rich's Richwhip (whipping "cream")
Solait Beverage Powder
Soyagen Soy Beverage Powder
Soyamel
Soy Moo by Health Valley
Vitamite Nondairy Milk Substitute

*Cheese Substitutes*

Galaxy Foods produces: *Formagg* Cheese Substitute
   Products: Lactose-Free Cheese Product made from Casein
   (milk protein) Mozzarella, Provolone, Cheddar, Swiss,
   American, Parmesan, Romano, Cottage, Ricotta,
   Monterey Jack
*Soymage Casein-Free Cheese Alternative* (also lactose free)
   Mozarella, Cheddar, Jalapeno, Monterey Jack
*Friendship* Foods Lactose-Reduced Lowfat Cottage Cheese
   (available in New York/New Jersey area and Florida)
*Lactaid Lactose*—Reduced American Processed & Cottage
   Cheese

*Milk-Free Margarine*

Blue Bonnet Diet
Diet Imperial
Fleischmann's Unsalted

Maneschewitz
Marv-Parv
Mazola Salt-Free
Parkay Light
Purity
Shedd's Spread Country Crock
Weight Watchers'

Write to these companies about products available in your area:

### MANUFACTURERS OF LACTOSE-FREE PRODUCTS

| COMPANY | PRODUCT |
|---|---|
| Barricini Foods<br>123 South Street<br>Oyster Bay, NY 11771 | Tofulite |
| Brightsong Light Foods<br>P.O. Box 2536<br>Petaluma, CA 94953 | Diet DeLite<br>Spicy Skinny Dip<br>Lite 'n Creamy Non-Dairy Dessert<br>LeTofu Frozen Dessert |
| Castle and Cook Inc.<br>50 California Street<br>San Francisco, CA 94111 | Dole Fruit Sorbet<br>Dole Fruit 'N Juice Bars |
| Eden Foods<br>701 Clinton Tecumseh Hwy.<br>Clinton, MI 49236 | Soy Milks |
| Ener-G Foods<br>6901 Fox Avenue South<br>P.O. Box 24723<br>Seattle, WA 98124 | Jolly Joan Soy Milk Powder |
| Farm Foods, Inc.<br>123 South Street<br>Oyster Bay, NY 11771 | Ice Bean Sandwiches<br>Ice Bean |
| Friendship Foods, Inc.<br>4900 Maspeth Avenue<br>Maspeth, NY 11378 | Lowfat Cottage Cheese<br>  (Lactose reduced) |

Galaxy Cheese Company
RD 3
North Gate Industrial Park
New Castle, PA 16105

Formagg Lactose-Free Cheese
Soymage Lactose-Free and
    Casein-Free Cheese

Giant Food, Inc.
P.O. Box 1804
Washington, DC 20013

Dreamy Tofu Frozen Dessert

Health Valley Foods
700 Union Street
Montebello, CA 90640

Soy-Moo

Hosoda Brothers, Inc.
1444 Tennessee
San Francisco, CA 94107

Pudding Mixture
Koya Tofu

Imagine Foods, Inc.
Jamestown, MO 65046

Rice Dream

Lactaid, Inc.
P.O. Box 111
Pleasantville, NJ 08232

Lactose-Reduced Milk
Lactose-Reduced CalciMilk
    (calcium enriched)
Lactose-Reduced Cottage Cheese
Lactose-Reduced American
    Processed Cheese

Loma Linda Foods
11503 Pierce Street
Riverside, CA 92515

Soyagen

Mama Tish's Gourmet Sorbetto
5245 N. Rose Street
Rosemont, IL 60018

Sorbet

Midwest Distribution Group
2478 E. Oakton Street
Arlington Heights, IL 60005

Vitari Ice Cream/Bars

Miller Farms Foods Co., Inc.
Cedar Falls, IA 50613

Solait Beverage Powder

Morinaga Nutritional Foods
5800 S. Eastern Ave. #270
Los Angeles, CA 90040

Tofu (Soft and Firm)

Nasoya Foods, Inc.
23 Jytek Drive
P.O. Box 841
Leominster, MA 01453

Creamy Tofu Dressing

Old Uncle Gaylord's                      Fruit Ices
824 Petaluma Blvd. South
Petaluma, CA 94952

Pevely Dairy                             Vitarich
1001 South Grand Blvd.
St. Louis, MO 63104

Presto Food Products, Inc.               Mocha Mix Non-Dairy
P.O. Box 584                                 Frozen Dessert
City of Industry, CA 91747

Simex International                      D'Best Frozen Coconut Milk
3 Dorman Ave.
San Francisco, CA 94124

Tofu Time, Inc.                          Tofutti
1638 63rd Street
Brooklyn, NY 11204

Tuscan Dairies                           Tofu Pops
750 Union
Union, NY 07083

Valley Rich                              Enjoy Lowfat Milk
Roanoke, VA                              70% Lactose Reduced

Westbrae Natural Foods                   Vanilla Malted
Emeryville, CA 94608

Worthington Foods, Inc.                  Soyamel
900 Proprietors Road
Worthington, OH 43085

For complete information about baby foods write to:

Gerber Products Company
Fremont, MI 49412

Heinz USA
Consumer Relations Department
Pittsburgh, PA 15230

Medical Services Department
The Beech-Nut Nutrition Corporation
Fort Washington, PA 19034

# 7

# Managing in the Pharmacy

L iterally thousands of prescription and over-the-counter medications and vitamin supplements contain lactose and must be avoided. Lactose is used as a filler in many medicines, often added to make the tablet the manufacturer's specified size. It is not a problem for the person who takes medicines occasionally, but for millions of people who do take vitamins or need to take prescription drugs, including birth control pills, every day or several days a week, the lactose content could cause difficulty.

Identifying medications that contain lactose is not always easy. Legally, there have been very few changes in the way that food and drugs, both prescription and over-the-counter, are labeled. In fact, there have been no statutory changes made since 1956. However, many recommendations have been made to drug companies by the Food and Drug Administration in response to consumer demand for better labeling. All of these are strictly voluntary. They are not followed up by the FDA or policed in any way. If manufacturers choose to improve their labels and give complete disclosure, they do so out of respect for the consumer. Therefore, companies that provide complete ingredient information should be contacted, thanked, and patronized.

Over-the-counter medications and prescription drugs will usually list their ingredients in two categories: active and inactive. The "active" ingredients are those that do the job of the medicine. The "inactive" ingredients include colorings, flavorings, and fillers to make the medicine palatable or usable. You will find lactose listed under "inactive ingredients." Here, too, it does not have to be listed specifically; it may be called "sugar."

We should be seeing better labeling from pharmaceutical companies, though. Three associations of drug manufacturers have decided to voluntarily list all ingredients on their labels. They are the Pharmaceutical Manufacturers Association, the Generic Pharmaceutical Industry Association, and the Propriety Associations. Because drug manufacturers who are members of these three groups comprise the majority of suppliers in this country, we can look forward to more complete drug labeling than ever before.

If you still don't know whether something you are taking contains lactose, you may find out by:

1. Checking with your pharmacist.
2. Checking with your physician.
3. Going to the library and checking in the *Physician's Desk Reference.* There is a PDR for prescription drugs and one for over-the-counter drugs. Complete ingredient listing is voluntary.
4. Writing or calling the pharmaceutical company.

## LACTASE ENZYME PRODUCTS

There are several pharmaceutical companies that manufacture lactase enzyme products. These are used by many people with good results, although they should not be construed as the panacea for a lactose-intolerant condition. Lactase enzyme can be added to milk either in a liquid or powder form. It will break down the lactose content by 70 percent. Doubled, it may break down the lactose by up to 90 percent. Lactase enzyme comes in tablet form also, allowing you to chew a few tablets just before eating small quantities of dairy foods. Using enzymes supplements can be wonderful for some people who have a limited lactose intolerance. They have also been used by nursing mothers for their infants and even by small children. If it works for you, the benefits will be great because you may now have a daily dose of calcium-rich dairy food, allowing you to possibly give up mineral supplementation. But while this type of lactase enzyme replacement works well, it isn't perfect.

As you already know, several dairy foods in the marketplace come pre-treated with lactase enzyme. You may treat your own food at home or experiment with chewable enzyme tablets. Look for the following products in your neighborhood pharmacy or health food store. Write to these companies for more information:

"Lactaid" produced by
Lactaid Inc.
P.O. Box 111
Pleasantville, NJ 08232
Hot Line: 1-800-257-8650

"Lacteeze Drops"
Kingsmill Foods Ltd.
1399 Kennedy Road Unit 17
Scarborough, Ontario
Canada M1P 2L6

"Lactrase" produced by
Kremers-Urban Pharmaceuticals
P.O. Box 2038
Milwaukee, WI 53201

"Milk Digestant"
Natural Sales Company
P.O. Box 25
Pittsburgh, PA 15230

Schiff Bio-Foods
121 Moonachie Avenue
Moonachie, NJ 07074

# 8

# Dining Out

eing lactose intolerant or milk allergic should not stop you from enjoying a meal out in a restaurant. There are many exciting choices out there, and restaurants are getting more and more accustomed to having patrons order food prepared in a special way. There is nothing unusual or rude about asking for your food to be prepared without dairy products if possible. Here are a few guidelines:

1. Before you order, ask if the dish you want is made with milk, butter, or cheese.
2. If it is, see if they can be omitted.
3. Order your toast dry, with jelly; your salad or sandwich without cheese; your meat, poultry, or fish broiled dry rather than sautéed in butter.
4. Don't be shy about telling the waiter that you don't wish to have any dairy products in your meal because you are sensitive to them.
5. Choose simple foods—salads, broiled entrees, boiled or baked potato (without sour cream or butter), steamed vegetables without melted butter.
6. You will most likely have to skip dessert, although occasionally you may select from: fruit pies, angel food cake, pecan pie, lemon meringue pie, pears zagablione, or fresh fruit.

7. Soups can be tricky. Minestrone usually has Romano or Parmesan cheese, tomato soup is often prepared with milk, and creamed soups are definitely out. Chicken or beef-broth-based soups should be fine.
8. Salad dressings that are safe: vinaigrette without cheese, Thousand Island, French, vinegar and oil. Ranch is made with buttermilk, creamy garlic is often made with sour cream, and Bleu cheese is exactly what it claims to be.
9. You may have to avoid French restaurants where butter and cream dominate the dishes. Also, your choices in an Italian restaurant will be *very* slim. Likewise Mexican, because just about everything is prepared with cheese. Instead, look for American or ethnic restaurants and the new light cuisine restaurants that feature grilled meats and fish with steamed fresh vegetables.

Here are a few choices of menu items at various kinds of restaurants:

*Cajun:*   Blackened Fish, Red Beans and Rice, Gumbo Soup, Jambalaya, Shrimp Creole, Grilled Catfish
*Chinese:*   Enjoy them all. Chinese cooking is milk free.
*French:*   Chateaubriand, Bouillabaisse, Ratatouille, Beef Bourguignon
*Greek:*   Stuffed Grape Leaves, Gyro (without yogurt), Greek Salad (without Feta cheese)
*Indian:*   Indian food is generally milk free.
*Italian:*   Pasta with Marinara Sauce, Green Salad, Bread Sticks, Chicken Cacciatore, Melon Proscuitto
*Japanese:*   Japanese food is generally milk free.
*Mexican:*   Fajitas (without sour cream), Guacamole, Flautas, Refried Beans, Taco (without cheese), Taco Salad (without cheese or sour cream), Tortilla Chips, Salsa, Picante Sauce, Chili, Gazpacho
*Middle Eastern:*   Schwarmas, Pita Bread, Hummus, Tabouli Salad, Tahina, Dolma, Lentil Salad, Couscous, Rice Pilaf, Shish-Kebab

*Spanish:*   Huevos Rancheros, Paella
*Szechuan:*   Szechuan cooking is milk free. It is prepared with
  a variety of hot peppers and tangy spices that may be
  irritating to some.

## FAST FOOD RESTAURANTS

Wanting to know about the dairy content of various fast foods,
I wrote to several large chains and received prompt and helpful
information from almost all of them. They sent me detailed
information regarding their products, the ingredients they use,
and nutritional information including calories per serving,
sodium content, cholesterol content, and purchasing information. I have included the addresses of the restaurant chains so
that you may write and receive this information for yourself if
you wish. Often, the restaurants have nutrition booklets available on the premises, so you may want to check there first.

It is important to remember that sugar is a common ingredient in many processed foods, and sometimes lactose is used in
place of or along with dextrose or sucrose. However, it does
look as though the majority of these restaurants use dextrose as
their sugar ingredient. A few simple guidelines: avoid breaded
foods, or at least remove the breading before eating, order all
burgers without cheese, and read all labels of salad dressing
packages.

Baskin-Robbins
P.O. Box 1200
Glendale, CA 91209

All sorbets and ices are milk free. Check with your local Baskin-
Robbins proprietor for varieties.

Daquiri Ice
Grape Ice
Lime Ice
Raspberry Sorbet
Boysenberry Sorbet

Burger King
P.O. Box 520783
General Mail Facility
Miami, FL 33152

*Milk-Free Items:*

Hamburger Buns
Whopper/Burger Patty is 100 percent beef
Chicken Specialty
Ham, Sausage, and Bacon
All Condiments
Tartar Sauce
Barbecue Sauce
Horseradish Sauce
Sweet and Sour Sauce
French Fries
Hash Browns
Thousand Island Dressing
Reduced-Calorie Italian Dressing

*These items contain milk or lactose:*

All dishes with cheese
Croissant contains skim milk.
Whaler Fish Fillet is battered with whey.
Chicken Tenders are battered with buttermilk.
Onion Rings are battered with whey.
French Toast Sticks contain non-fat dry milk.
Eggs are mixed with whole milk.
Great Danish contains skim milk.
House Dressing contains buttermilk.
Apple Pie contains casein.


Dunkin' Donuts
587 Granite Street
Braintree, MA 02184

*Milk-Free Items:*

There may be some items at your local Dunkin' Donuts that are milk free. Take this list with you and see if you can locate something acceptable.

*These items contain milk or lactose:*

All Cookies
All Cake Donut Products
All Yeast-Raised Donut Products
Corn Muffins
Blueberry Muffins
Cranberry-Orange Muffins
Apple Muffins
Pumpkin Muffins
Cherry Muffins
Banana Muffins
Buttercreme Filling
Croissants


Hardee's Food Systems, Inc.
1233 N. Church Street
P.O. Box 1619
Rocky Mount, NC 27802-1619

Hardee's did not provide ingredient listings for their products. However, they did provide a list of various nutrients in their foods with Calcium as a category. Based on the amount of calcium in various products, we can guess the milk content. The following items showed a large calcium content and should be avoided:

Cheeseburger (125 mg)
Quarter Pound Cheeseburger (194 mg)
Big Deluxe (150 mg)
Bacon Cheeseburger (146 mg)
Mushroom n' Swiss (111 mg)
Roast Beef Sandwich (85 mg)

Hot Ham n' Cheese (207 mg)
Fisherman's Fillet (139 mg)
Chicken Fillet (83 mg)
Hot Dog (44 mg)
Milkshake (450 mg)
Ham Biscuit with Egg (211 mg)
Sausage Biscuit with Egg (169 mg)
Steak Biscuit (120 mg)
Ham Biscuit (181 mg)
Biscuit (150 mg)

The following items show a very small calcium content and may be considered acceptable:

Turkey Club (39 mg)
Chef Salad (if eaten without the cheese)
French Fries (13 mg)
Apple Turnover (19 mg)
Big Cookie (16 mg)
One Medium Fried Egg (30 mg)
Hamburger (23 mg)


Jack in the Box
Foodmaker, Inc.
P.O. Box 783
9330 Balboa Avenue
San Diego, CA 92112

*Milk-Free Items:*

| | |
|---|---|
| Apple Turnover | Hamburger Buns |
| Barbecue Sauce | Hamburger Seasoning |
| Bacon | Hashbrowns |
| Beef Patty | Kaiser Roll |
| Breakfast Ham | All Condiments |
| Canadian Style Bacon | Mushroom Topping |
| English Muffin | Mayo-Onion Sauce |
| French Fries | Onion Bun |
| Gourm-Egg | Pancake Syrup |

Pasta Salad
Pita Bread
Rye Bread
Shrimp
Salsa
Seafood Cocktail Sauce
Secret Sauce
Tartar Sauce

Tortilla Chips
Tortilla Shell and Meat Filling
Turkey
Vegetable Shortening
Wedge Fries
Wheat Bun
Whitefish and Crab Blend

*These items contain milk or lactose:*

Breaded Chicken Patty contains whey and non-fat milk.
Breaded Chicken Breast Strips contain whey and non-fat
    dry milk.
Breaded Fish Portions contain whey.
Breaded Onion Rings contain dried whey and skim
    milk powder.
Breaded Shrimp contains whey and non-fat dry milk.
House Dressing contains buttermilk.
Croissant contains non-fat dry milk and butter.
Garlic Roll contains mozzarella cheese.
Pancake Mix contains buttermilk.
Pork Sausage does contain sugar. May be lactose.
Sirloin Steak contains sugar and fillers. May contain lactose.
Taco Salad Meat contains sugar. May contain lactose.

Kentucky Fried Chicken
P.O. Box 32070
Louisville, KY 40232-2070

*These items contain milk or lactose:*

Original Recipe Chicken is dipped in milk and egg.
Kentucky Nuggets, Chicken Livers, and Chicken Sandwich
    are all prepared with milk.
Extra-Crispy-Chicken batter mix contains milk.

Mashed Potatoes include whey solids.
Biscuits are made with buttermilk and margarine.
Desserts contain milk.


McDonald's
McDonald's Plaza
Oakbrook, IL 60521

*Milk-Free Items:*

Big Mac (without cheese)     Chef Salad (without cheese)
Beef Patty                   Shrimp Salad (without cheese)
Hamburger Bun                Side Salad
All Condiments               Salad Dressing ingredients vary.
French Fries                 Please read the labels.
Big Mac Sauce
Barbecue Sauce
Bacon

*These items contain milk or lactose:*

Biscuits are made with buttermilk.
Danish, Cakes, and Cookies all contain milk.
Fish Sandwich may be breaded with milk products.
Chicken McNuggets may be breaded with milk products.
All cheese dishes


Wendy's International
P.O. Box 256
4288 West Dublin Granville Road
Dublin, OH 43017

*Milk-Free Items:*

Hamburger Patties            Non-Dairy Creamer is
Hamburger Buns                  available
Bacon                        Chicken Nugget Sauces may
All Condiments                  vary

Chili
French Fries
Salad Bar
Bread Sticks
Cole Slaw
Celery Seed Dressing
French Dressing
Golden Italian Dressing
Thousand Island Dressing
Reduced-Calorie Italian
   Dressing

Fish Fillet
Taco Salad without cheese or
   sour cream
Tartar Sauce
French Toast
Breakfast Potatoes
Sausage Patty
Syrup
Wheat Toast contains molasses
Liquid Margarine

*These items contain milk or lactose:*

All Sandwiches with Cheese
Chicken Breast Fillet is battered with skim milk and whey.
All Baked Potato Dishes are made with Cheese Sauce.
Chicken Nuggets are battered with buttermilk.
Croutons contain Romano Cheese and whey.
Pasta Salad contains Romano Cheese.
Ranch Dressing contains buttermilk.
Reduced-Calorie Bacon/Tomato Dressing contains skim
   milk.
Reduced-Calorie Creamy Cucumber Dressing contains sour
   cream and milk.
Reduced-Calorie Thousand Island Dressing contains non-fat
   milk.
Whipped Margarine contains whey.
Multi-Grain Bun contains molasses.
All omelets contain cheese.
Buttermilk Biscuit contains non-fat milk.
Sausage Gravy contains sodium caseinate.
Wheat Toast contains molasses.
White Toast contains non-fat milk.

# Recipes

## The Complete Dairy-Free Diet

### DAIRY PRODUCTS

The following contain dairy products and are to be avoided:

2% Milk
1% Milk
½% Milk
Acidophilus Milk
Butter
Buttermilk
Cheese
Condensed Milk
Cream
Cream Cheese
Custard
Evaporated Milk
Goat's Milk
Half and Half
Ice Cream
Ice Milk
Lowfat Milk
Margarine
"Non-Dairy" Products

Powdered Milk
Pudding
Sherbet
Skim Milk
Sour Cream
Whole Milk
Yogurt

On product labels look for and avoid:

Lactoglobulin
Casein
Lactalbumin          } (milk proteins)
Sodium Caseinate
Whey (contains both milk protein and milk sugar)
Lactose (milk sugar)

# Dishes Prepared with Milk

The following dishes are prepared with milk and are to be avoided (unless safely prepared at home):

Au Gratin Potatoes
Bavarian Cream
Bisques
Breaded Meats and Seafood
Breaded Vegetables
Butter Sauce
Cheese Sauce
Chowder
Cream Pie
Cream Sauce
Creamy Casseroles
Creamed Eggs
Creamed Soups
Creamy Salad Dressing
Eggnog
Macaroni and Cheese
Mousse
Omelettes
Pancakes and Crepes
Pasta with Sauce
Scalloped Potatoes
Twice-Baked Potatoes
Waffles

# Baked Goods

The following baked goods are prepared with milk and are to be avoided (unless safely prepared at home):

| | |
|---|---|
| Biscuits | Packaged Breads, Rolls |
| Cookies | Cakes |
| Crackers | Pie Crust |
| Donuts | Pie Filling |

# Sweets

The following sweets are made with milk and are to be avoided (unless safely prepared at home):

Baked Goods from a Bakery or Patisserie
Cakes and Cookies
Cheese Cakes
Cream Filled Cakes
Cream Pie
Croissants
Milk Chocolate
Strudels, Coffee Cakes
White Chocolate
Exception: *Pareve* items in a kosher bakery are all prepared
    without milk products and are acceptable on a dairy-free diet.

# Processed Foods

Dried milk is a common ingredient found in many processed meats including:

| | |
|---|---|
| Bologna | Salami |
| Hot Dogs | Sausage |
| Pepperoni | |

Exception: Kosher meat products are completely milk free.

# Packaged Foods

Dried milk is often found in these mixes:

Cake Mix                    Instant Potatoes
Coating Mix for Chicken     "Helper" Dishes
Cookie Mix                  Rehydratable Foods

# Acceptable Foods

Although it may seem like the list of forbidden foods is endless, what's left is quite sufficient around which to build wonderful meals and exciting menus. The marketplace is full of milk-free items, some developed especially for people with lactose intolerance or milk-protein allergy. You will be able to choose from many milk-free desserts, "ice creams," breads, meats, and prepared foods. Your vegetables and fruits will be fresh and nutritionally superior. Check chapter six for a list of milk-free foods in the marketplace.

Build your menus around the following:

Air Cakes—Angel Food, Sponge Cake, Jelly Roll
Bouillon, Broth-Based Soups
Condiments including Mayonaisse, Mustard, Ketchup
Fish and Seafood
Fresh Fruits
Fresh Vegetables
Frozen Juice Desserts
Jams, Honey
Kosher-Pareve Items
Lactose-reduced Milk, Cheese, and Ice Cream
Lean Beef/Veal
Marshmallows, Fruit Candies, Licorice, Dark Chocolate
Milk-Free Margarines
Milk-Free Milk Substitutes
Milk-Free Whipped Cream
Pasta
Potatoes
Poultry
Rice
Tofu-based Ice Creams

# Appetizers

## Anchovy Puffs

*Makes 4 Servings, 3 puffs each*

Plain pastry (2 9-inch pie shells, homemade or prepared)
2-ounce can of anchovies

Mash anchovies and blend into pastry mixture. Roll to ¼-inch thickness. Cut into squares or other shapes. Place on an ungreased cookie sheet. Bake at 450° for 10 minutes or until puffs are nicely browned.

| Each serving provides: | | | |
|---|---|---|---|
| 396 | Calories | 33 g | Carbohydrate |
| 6 g | Protein | 481 mg | Sodium |
| 27 g | Fat | 3 mg | Cholesterol |

# Stuffed Mushrooms

*Makes 8 Servings*

1   pound fresh mushrooms
2   tablespoons chives, chopped
2   tablespoons milk-free margarine
2   eggs (or substitute), beaten
2   teaspoons salt
1   teaspoon pepper
1   teaspoon garlic powder
Milk-free breadcrumbs
½   pound Italian sausage (optional)

Rinse mushrooms and pat dry with paper towel. Remove stems and chop. Set aside the caps. Sauté chives and chopped stems in margarine for 1 minute. Put this mixture in a small bowl. In the same pan, sauté Italian sausage, if using this ingredient. Drain fat. Add to the sautéed mushrooms in small bowl. To the mushrooms add eggs, salt, pepper, and garlic powder. Blend thoroughly. Spoon mixture into mushroom caps and sprinkle with bread crumbs. Place mushrooms on an ungreased cookie sheet. Bake at 425° for about 15 minutes or until bread crumbs are browned.

| Each serving (with sausage) provides: | | | |
|---|---|---|---|
| 74 | Calories | 6 g | Carbohydrate |
| 3 g | Protein | 627 mg | Sodium |
| 5 g | Fat | 69 mg | Cholesterol |

# Shrimp Croustades

*Makes 16 Servings, 1 croustade each*

16 slices milk-free bread  Milk-free margarine
Shrimp filling  Milk-free bread crumbs

Cut out 16 rounds of bread with the top of a 3-inch glass. Reserve the crusts for making bread crumbs. Place rounds in the cups of a muffin pan and press them into shape. Bake at 375° for 10 minutes. Remove toasted rounds and place them on a cookie sheet. Fill each with a hefty spoonful of shrimp filling. Top with a dot of milk-free margarine and sprinkle with bread crumbs. Bake at 450° for 10 minutes or until toasted. Serve hot.

# Shrimp Filling

1 8-ounce bag of tiny frozen shrimp or 2 cups fresh, cooked shrimp (other type of firm fish may be substituted)

3 tablespoons mayonnaise

3 tablespoons chili sauce

1½ tablespoons minced onion

8 drops tabasco sauce

2 tablespoons minced celery

2 teaspoons lemon juice

Toss all ingredients together.

| Each serving provides: | | | |
|---|---|---|---|
| 171 | Calories | 25 g | Carbohydrate |
| 7 g | Protein | 351 mg | Sodium |
| 5 g | Fat | 31 mg | Cholesterol |

# Guacamole

*Makes 4 Servings*

2    avocados (pitted and peeled)
1    tablespoon grated onion
1    tablespoon lemon juice
1    chopped tomato
½    teaspoon chili powder

Mash avocado with a fork. Blend in other ingredients and mix well. Chill for at least 30 minutes for flavors to blend. Serve with corn chips.

| | Each serving provides: | | |
|---|---|---|---|
| 170 | Calories | 9 g | Carbohydrate |
| 2 g | Protein | 7 mg | Sodium |
| 16 g | Fat | 00 mg | Cholesterol |

# Hot n' Spicy Salsa

*Makes 4 Servings*

| | |
|---|---|
| 2 | ripe tomatoes, peeled and seeded |
| ½ | Bermuda onion |
| ½ | green pepper |
| ½ | red pepper |
| 1 | medium jalapeño pepper |
| | Juice of one lime |
| 1 | garlic clove, minced |
| 1 | teaspoon parsley |

Dice tomatoes, onion, and peppers. Put in a bowl and add the lime, garlic, and parsley. Blend well. Let stand at room temperature at least 2 hours for flavors to blend. Serve with blue tortilla corn chips.

---

Each serving provides:

| 31 | Calories | 7 g | Carbohydrate |
|---|---|---|---|
| 1 g | Protein | 7 mg | Sodium |
| .27 g | Fat | 00 mg | Cholesterol |

# Pico de Gallo

*Makes 8 Servings*

1   6-ounce can black olives, chopped
1   4-ounce can green chilies, chopped
4   ripe tomatoes, chopped
8   green onions, chopped
2   tablespoons olive oil
1   tablespoon vinegar
3   teaspoons garlic salt

Combine all ingredients. Chill for at least one hour so that the flavors can blend. Serve with corn chips.

|  |  |  |  |
|---|---|---|---|
| | Each serving provides: | | |
| 90 | Calories | 6 g | Carbohydrate |
| 1 g | Protein | 943 mg | Sodium |
| 8 g | Fat | 00 mg | Cholesterol |

# Bologna en Croute

*Makes 8 Servings*

1   prepared pie crust pastry
3   tablespoons prepared mustard
1   small (1 pound) kosher bologna
1   egg

Spread mustard on the pie crust. Remove the plastic wrap from the bologna and set bologna in the center of the crust. Wrap the pastry around the meat and seal bottom and ends with water. Beat egg with 1 tablespoon water. Brush on pastry. Bake at 350° until golden brown, about 30 minutes. Slice and serve.

| Each serving provides: | | | |
|---|---|---|---|
| 384 | Calories | 18 g | Carbohydrate |
| 10 g | Protein | 787 mg | Sodium |
| 30 g | Fat | 66 mg | Cholesterol |

# Tempting Teriyaki

*Makes 4 Servings*

| | |
|---|---|
| 1 | tablespoon chopped onion |
| 1 | clove minced garlic |
| 1 | teaspoon Worcestershire sauce |
| ¼ | cup soy sauce |
| 1 | tablespoon sugar |
| ¼ | teaspoon ground ginger |
| 1 | pound sirloin steak, cut into thin strips |
| 1 | 6-ounce can sliced water chestnuts |

In a small bowl, combine onion, garlic, Worcestershire sauce, soy sauce, sugar, and ginger. Add steak strips and toss. Let meat marinate 30 minutes or longer. Drain the sirloin strips and wrap each around two water chestnuts. Fasten with a toothpick. Broil until done, turning once. May be microwaved about 3 minutes on full power.

| Each serving provides: | | | |
|---|---|---|---|
| 310 | Calories | 8 g | Carbohydrate |
| 21 g | Protein | 596 mg | Sodium |
| 21 g | Fat | 72 mg | Cholesterol |

# Crudités

*Makes 6 Servings*

4   carrots, peeled and sliced into 3-inch strips
4   stalks celery, peeled and cut into 3-inch strips
¼   cauliflower, cut off ends, break apart into flowerets
2   small zucchini, cut into 3-inch strips

# Dip

⅓   cup mayonnaise
½   cup ketchup
¼   cup sweet pickle relish
4   drops tabasco

Prepare vegetables. Keep crisp in cold water in the refrigerator until serving time. Blend all ingredients for dip and serve.

| Each serving provides: | | | |
|---|---|---|---|
| 268 | Calories | 17 g | Carbohydrate |
| 2 g | Protein | 513 mg | Sodium |
| 22 g | Fat | 16 mg | Cholesterol |

# Hummous

*Makes 4 Servings*

| | |
|---|---|
| 1 | 15-ounce can garbanzo beans, rinsed and drained |
| 2 | tablespoons chopped chives |
| 2 | cloves garlic, minced |
| 1 | tablespoon vegetable or olive oil |
| 3 | tablespoons lemon juice |
| ½ | teaspoon salt |
| ¼ | teaspoon white pepper |
| ½ | teaspoon dill |
| ¼ | cup water |

Place all ingredients in a food processor or blender. Purée, adding water if needed. Chill at least one hour before serving. Serve with triangles of pita bread.

---

Each serving provides:

| 162 | Calories | 25 g | Carbohydrate |
|---|---|---|---|
| 5 g | Protein | 594 mg | Sodium |
| 5 g | Fat | 00 mg | Cholesterol |

# Pineapple Rumaki

*Makes 4 Servings*

Chunks of fresh pineapple, or canned (drained well)

2    tablespoons soy sauce

½    teaspoon garlic salt

1    8-ounce can sliced water chestnuts

½    pound bacon

Marinate pineapple chunks in soy sauce for 30 minutes. Add garlic salt. Swish in the bowl. Remove and drain. Top each pineapple chunk with a water chestnut and wrap with ½ slice of bacon. Broil 2 minutes, turning once. Serve hot.

---

Each serving provides:

| 129 | Calories | 9 g | Carbohydrate |
|-----|----------|-----|--------------|
| 6 g | Protein | 573 mg | Sodium |
| 8 g | Fat | 13 mg | Cholesterol |

# Mississippi Caviar

*Makes 8 Servings*

2     15-ounce cans black-eyed peas
1     cup salad oil
½     cup red wine vinegar
1     clove garlic, peeled and cut into fourths
¼     cup chopped green onions
5     drops tabasco sauce

Drain peas. Add remaining ingredients and stir well. Store in refrigerator at least 3 days. After first day, remove garlic. Serve with wide corn chips.

| Each serving provides: | | | |
|---|---|---|---|
| 326 | Calories | 15 g | Carbohydrate |
| 5 g | Protein | 318 mg | Sodium |
| 28 g | Fat | 00 mg | Cholesterol |

# Microwaved Buffalo Wings

*Makes 12 Servings*

2-3  pounds chicken wings

12  ounces apricot preserves

6  ounces Russian salad dressing

1  package milk-free onion soup mix

Rinse chicken wings in cold water and snip off wing tips. Discard. Cut wings into their two component parts. Blend remaining ingredients and pour over chicken wings that have been arranged in a 2-quart microwaveable baking dish. Cook on full power for about 9 minutes or until nicely browned.

| | Each serving provides: | | |
|---|---|---|---|
| 278 | Calories | 23 g | Carbohydrate |
| 10 g | Protein | 380 mg | Sodium |
| 16 g | Fat | 40 mg | Cholesterol |

# Caviar Pie

*Makes 6 Servings*

6     hard-boiled eggs

1     tablespoon mayonnaise

2     2-3-ounce jars caviar (red or black)

½     cup Bermuda onion, chopped

Chop eggs thoroughly and mix with just enough mayonnaise to hold chopped eggs together. Press gently into a 6-inch springform pan. Refrigerate for several hours or overnight. Remove outside of pan and place egg mold on a serving dish. Spread top with a thin layer of mayonnaise, then a layer of caviar. Sprinkle with chopped onion. Refrigerate until serving time.

---

Each serving provides:

| 159 | Calories | 3 g | Carbohydrate |
|-----|----------|-----|--------------|
| 12 g | Protein | 437 mg | Sodium |
| 11 g | Fat | 414 mg | Cholesterol |

# Beverages

## Morning Nog

*Makes 1 Serving*

1    cup pineapple juice
1    tablespoon honey
3-6  ice cubes

Combine all ingredients in a blender until frothy. Serves one.

| Each serving provides: | | | |
|---|---|---|---|
| 194 | Calories | 49 g | Carbohydrate |
| 1 g | Protein | 4 mg | Sodium |
| .07 g | Fat | 00 mg | Cholesterol |

# Banana-Berry Breakfast

*Makes 2 Servings*

1    whole ripe banana
1    cup frozen berries
1    cup apple juice
3    ice cubes

Mix all ingredients together in a blender. Blend at medium speed until smooth.

| Each serving provides: | | | |
|---|---|---|---|
| 137 | Calories | 35 g | Carbohydrate |
| .97 g | Protein | 6 mg | Sodium |
| .48 g | Fat | 00 mg | Cholesterol |

# Hawaiian Sunrise

*Makes 2 Servings*

1    8-ounce can pineapple chunks in natural juice
¾    cup orange juice
4    maraschino cherries
3    ice cubes

Mix all ingredients together in a blender. Blend at high speed until frothy.

| Each serving provides: | | | |
|---|---|---|---|
| 116 | Calories | 29 g | Carbohydrate |
| 1 g | Protein | 2 mg | Sodium |
| .15 g | Fat | 00 mg | Cholesterol |

# Tangy Watermelon Cooler

*Makes 2 Servings*

¼    small watermelon
      Juice of 1 lemon
3     ice cubes

Remove the watermelon rind and any seeds. Cut the melon into chunks and purée in a blender. Add lemon juice and pour over ice to serve.

| Each serving provides: | | | |
|---|---|---|---|
| 106 | Calories | 24 g | Carbohydrate |
| 2 g | Protein | 7 mg | Sodium |
| 1 g | Fat | 00 mg | Cholesterol |

# Carrot Cocktail

*Makes 2 Servings*

1     8-ounce can sliced carrots       2    tablespoons water
½    cup orange juice                   2    ice cubes
¼    teaspoon cinnamon

Do not drain carrots. Instead, blend all the ingredients including the liquid from the can of carrots together at high speed until smooth.

| Each serving provides: | | | |
|---|---|---|---|
| 55 | Calories | 13 g | Carbohydrate |
| 1 g | Protein | 274 mg | Sodium |
| 23 g | Fat | 00 mg | Cholesterol |

# Lemon Float

*Makes 1 Serving*

1½    cups lemonade

1     scoop Milk-Free Vanilla Ice Cream

1     slice orange

Pour lemonade into a tall glass. Add ice cream and garnish with a slice of orange or lime. Makes a single serving.

| Each serving provides: | | | |
|---|---|---|---|
| 144 | Calories | 28 g | Carbohydrate |
| .56 g | Protein | 20 mg | Sodium |
| 4 g | Fat | 17 mg | Cholesterol |

# Hot Cocoa

*Makes 1 Serving*

½     cup milk substitute

½     cup water

1½    teaspoons cocoa powder

¾     teaspoon sugar

      Marshmallow for garnish

Put all ingredients in a small saucepan and warm over very low heat, stirring constantly. Pour into mug and garnish with a marshmallow.

| Each serving provides: | | | |
|---|---|---|---|
| 182 | Calories | 18 g | Carbohydrate |
| 2 g | Protein | 95 mg | Sodium |
| 12 g | Fat | 00 mg | Cholesterol |

# Faux Milk Shake

*Makes 2 Servings*

½   cup orange juice

½   cup milk substitute

1    banana

3-6  ice cubes

Put all ingredients in a blender and whip until frothy. Serve at once.

<table>
<tr><td colspan="4">Each serving provides:</td></tr>
<tr><td>162</td><td>Calories</td><td>27 g</td><td>Carbohydrate</td></tr>
<tr><td>2 g</td><td>Protein</td><td>49 mg</td><td>Sodium</td></tr>
<tr><td>6 g</td><td>Fat</td><td>00 mg</td><td>Cholesterol</td></tr>
</table>

# Holiday Punch

*Makes 16 Servings*

2  46-ounce cans pineapple juice
1  46-ounce can orange juice
1  quart ginger ale
1  half-gallon Light Strawberry Ice Cream
   Orange and lime slices for garnish

Put all ingredients in a punch bowl and stir. Add ice, and garnish with fruit.

---

|  | Each serving provides: | | |
|---|---|---|---|
| 241 | Calories | 51 g | Carbohydrate |
| 2 g | Protein | 36 mg | Sodium |
| 4 g | Fat | 17 mg | Cholesterol |

# Breads and Stuffings

## Quick-and-Easy Yeast Rolls

*Makes 16 Servings (1 per serving)*

| | |
|---|---|
| 1 | package active dry yeast |
| ¾ | cup warm water (105°-115°) |
| 2 | tablespoons sugar |
| 2 | tablespoons vegetable oil |
| ½ | teaspoon salt |
| 1 | egg, beaten lightly |
| 2½ | cups flour |

Dissolve yeast in water in a 2½-quart bowl. Add sugar, oil, salt and egg. Stir to dissolve sugar and salt. Stir in 1 cup flour until smooth. Cover with a cloth and place on rack over bowl of warm water. Let rise 15 minutes. Grease a square 9-inch pan. Stir down batter and add 1½ cups flour. Blend until mixed well and turn onto a floured, cloth-covered board. Knead 3 minutes. If sticky, knead in ¼ cup flour. Divide dough into 16 pieces and shape quickly into balls. Arrange in the pan and brush tops with softened margarine. Cover with cloth and place on a rack over bowl of hot water. Let rise 25 minutes. Preheat oven to 425°. Bake 12-15 minutes or until light brown. Remove from pan to wire rack to cool. Brush tops with melted margarine, if desired.

| Each serving provides: | | | |
|---|---|---|---|
| 99 | Calories | 17 g | Carbohydrate |
| 3 g | Protein | 74 mg | Sodium |
| 2 g | Fat | 17 mg | Cholesterol |

# Cinnamon Rolls

*Makes 12 Servings (1 roll per serving)*

| | |
|---|---|
| 1 | package active dry yeast |
| ½ | cup warm water |
| 3 | tablespoons sugar |
| ½ | teaspoon salt |
| 2 | tablespoons milk-free margarine, softened |
| 1 | egg, beaten lightly |
| 2-2½ | cups flour (unsifted) |
| ⅓ | cup melted milk-free margarine |
| ⅓ | cup sugar |
| 1 | teaspoon cinnamon |
| | Confectioners' Sugar Frosting |

Dissolve yeast in warm water. Beat in sugar, salt, margarine, egg, and 1 cup flour. Add enough flour to make a soft dough. On a floured board, knead dough 2 minutes and roll out to a 9 × 18-inch rectangle. Brush with melted margarine. Sprinkle with combined sugar and cinnamon. Roll up like a jelly roll. Seal sides firmly and cut into 12 equal pieces. Arrange in a greased 8-inch round pan. Cover with a damp cloth. Place covered rolls in a cold oven on a wire rack over a pan of boiling water. Let rolls rise 30 minutes. Uncover rolls; remove rack and pan of water. Turn oven to 375° and bake for 30-35 minutes. While rolls are warm, frost with Confectioners' Sugar Frosting. Yield: 12 Rolls.

| Each serving provides: | | | |
|---|---|---|---|
| 237 | Calories | 37 g | Carbohydrate |
| 4 g | Protein | 201 mg | Sodium |
| 9 g | Fat | 23 mg | Cholesterol |

# Refrigerator Rolls

*Makes 8 Rolls*

| | |
|---|---|
| 1 | package active dry yeast |
| ¼ | cup warm water |
| 1 | cup ginger ale |
| ¼ | cup sugar |
| ¼ | cup milk-free margarine |
| 1 | teaspoon salt |
| 3½ | cups flour |
| 1 | egg |
| ¼ | cup melted milk-free margarine |

Soften yeast in the warm water and set aside. Let cool to lukewarm. In a medium-size bowl, combine ginger ale, sugar, margarine, and salt. Add 1½ cups flour to this mixture and beat well. Beat in yeast and egg. Gradually add remaining flour, beating well. Place dough in a large greased bowl. Turn dough once to grease surface. Cover and chill overnight. Grease a 6-inch muffin pan. Form rolls by placing three 1-inch balls in each muffin cup and brush the top with melted margarine. Bake at 400° for 12-15 minutes.

| Each serving provides: | | | |
|---|---|---|---|
| 116 | Calories | 17 g | Carbohydrate |
| 3 g | Protein | 140 mg | Sodium |
| 4 g | Fat | 11 mg | Cholesterol |

# Date-Nut Bread

*Makes 8 Servings*

| | |
|---|---|
| 1 | 4-ounce package pitted dates, cut into thirds |
| 1 | cup boiling water |
| 1¾ | cups flour |
| 1 | teaspoon baking soda |
| 1 | cup sugar |
| | Dash salt |
| 1 | tablespoon milk-free margarine |
| 1 | beaten egg |
| 1 | teaspoon vanilla |
| ¾ | cup chopped nuts |

Preheat oven to 350°. Cover dates with boiling water and set aside. Sift the next four ingredients together in a mixing bowl. Mix in margarine and egg. Add date and water mixture. Stir until all is moistened. Stir in vanilla and nuts. Turn into a well-greased 9 × 5 × 3-inch loaf pan. Bake at 350° about 45 minutes.

May be made in two 16-ounce cans. Fill about ⅔ full of batter. Stand upright on a baking sheet. Bake at 350° for about 30 minutes.

| Each serving provides: | | | |
|---|---|---|---|
| 331 | Calories | 59 g | Carbohydrate |
| 6 g | Protein | 147 mg | Sodium |
| 9 g | Fat | 34 mg | Cholesterol |

# Banana Muffins

*Makes 12 Servings (1 per serving)*

½  cup milk-free margarine
1   cup sugar
2   eggs
1   cup mashed banana
¾   teaspoon baking soda
½   teaspoon salt
1   cup flour

Grease one 12-cup muffin pan, or use paper inserts. Cream margarine and sugar. Add eggs, beating well, and stir in banana. Sift together dry ingredients. Add to banana mixture and mix well. Pour into greased muffin cups and bake at 350° for 25-30 minutes. Yield: 12 muffins.

|  | Each serving provides: | | |
|---|---|---|---|
| 201 | Calories | 29 g | Carbohydrate |
| 3 g | Protein | 244 mg | Sodium |
| 9 g | Fat | 46 mg | Cholesterol |

# Blueberry Muffins

*Makes 12 Servings (1 per serving)*

1½    cups flour

½     cup sugar

2     teaspoons baking powder

½     teaspoon salt

1     egg, well-beaten

½     cup water

⅓     cup melted milk-free margarine

1     cup fresh blueberries

Confectioners' sugar

Grease one 12-cup muffin pan, or use paper inserts. Combine dry ingredients. In a small bowl, combine egg, water, and margarine. Make a well in the center of the dry ingredients and add egg mixture all at once. Stir with a fork until just moist. Gently fold in blueberries. Fill muffin cups ⅔ full and bake at 400° for 25-30 minutes. Sprinkle tops with confectioners' sugar, if desired. Yield: 12 muffins.

| Each serving provides: | | | |
|---|---|---|---|
| 148 | Calories | 22 g | Carbohydrate |
| 3 g | Protein | 228 mg | Sodium |
| 6 g | Fat | 23 mg | Cholesterol |

# Milk-Free Bread Crumbs

Keep a plastic bag of milk-free bread crusts, ends, leftover rolls, and other odd pieces of bread in the freezer. When you have accumulated a considerable amount, transfer the bread to a large bowl. Let the pieces of bread sit at room temperature, uncovered, for several days. When all the bread is hard, put it through a blender, food processor, electric grater, or meat grinder. Store the crumbs in a covered container. Bread crumbs taste best when a variety of breads and rolls are used together. Add herbs or spices if you wish. Refrigerate for a longer shelf life.

# Beautiful Croutons

¼ cup milk-free margarine

½ teaspoon garlic salt

2 cups cubed French or Italian bread (1-inch cubes)

Melt margarine in a small skillet and add garlic salt. Sauté bread cubes in margarine mixture, turning, to brown on all sides. These croutons may be stored at room temperature for several hours.

| Each serving provides: | | | |
|---|---|---|---|
| 73 | Calories | 4 g | Carbohydrate |
| .74 g | Protein | 225 mg | Sodium |
| 6 g | Fat | .22 mg | Cholesterol |

# Orange-Nut Bread

*Makes 8 Servings*

| | |
|---|---|
| 1½ | cups flour |
| ½ | cup sugar |
| 2 | teaspoons baking powder |
| ½ | teaspoon salt |
| ¼ | cup melted milk-free margarine |
| 2 | eggs (or substitute) |
| ½ | cup orange juice |
| ¼ | cups chopped nuts |

Combine flour, sugar, baking powder, and salt. In a small bowl, combine the margarine, eggs, and orange juice, and add to the dry ingredients. Mix well and pour into a greased 1-quart loaf pan. Let mixture sit at room temperature for 15 minutes. Sprinkle nuts on top. Bake at 325° 1 hour or until toothpick inserted in center comes out clean.

---

Each serving provides:

| 236 | Calories | 33 g | Carbohydrate |
|---|---|---|---|
| 5 g | Protein | 329 mg | Sodium |
| 9 g | Fat | 69 mg | Cholesterol |

# Pull-Apart Onion Bread

*Makes 12 Servings*

1    large loaf milk-free French or Italian bread

1    small minced onion

½    cup milk-free margarine

½    teaspoon paprika

Cut diagonal slices into but not through the bread at 2-inch intervals. Sauté onion in margarine over very low heat; sprinkle paprika onto onion. Spoon about 1 tablespoon of onion mixture onto each diagonal cut in the bread. Wrap entire loaf in foil. Place in oven and heat at 350° for 15 minutes.

| Each serving provides: | | | |
|---|---|---|---|
| 179 | Calories | 21 g | Carbohydrate |
| 3 g | Protein | 309 mg | Sodium |
| 9 g | Fat | 1 mg | Cholesterol |

# Garlic Bread

*Makes 12 Servings*

½   teaspoon garlic powder
2    cloves crushed garlic
¼   cup melted milk-free margarine
1    large loaf milk-free French bread

In a small skillet, add garlic to melted margarine. Cut bread lengthwise into 2 pieces and spread with garlic-"butter" mixture. Place under the broiler for 5 watchful minutes.

| Each serving provides: | | | |
|---|---|---|---|
| 145 | Calories | 21 g | Carbohydrate |
| 3 g | Protein | 264 mg | Sodium |
| 5 g | Fat | 1 mg | Cholesterol |

# Dill Toast

*Makes 4 Servings*

8    pieces of thinly sliced bread
4    tablespoons milk-free margarine, softened
4    tablespoons freshly snipped dill

Remove crusts of bread. Combine margarine and dill. Spread on the tops of the bread. Bake at 300° for 15 minutes or until nicely browned. Goes well with soup.

| Each serving provides: | | | |
|---|---|---|---|
| 186 | Calories | 16 g | Carbohydrate |
| 3 g | Protein | 300 mg | Sodium |
| 12 g | Fat | 1 mg | Cholesterol |

# Golden Corn Bread

*Makes 4 Servings*

| | |
|---|---|
| 1 | cup corn meal |
| 1 | cup flour |
| ¼ | cup sugar |
| 4 | teaspoons baking powder |
| ¼ | teaspoon salt |
| 1 | cup milk substitute |
| 1 | egg |
| ¼ | cup vegetable oil |

Combine corn meal, flour, sugar, baking powder, salt. Add milk substitute, egg, and oil. Beat for one minute. Bake in a greased 8-inch pan in a preheated 425° oven for about 20 minutes. Serve warm.

---

Each serving provides:

| | | | |
|---|---|---|---|
| 513 | Calories | 71 g | Carbohydrate |
| 8 g | Protein | 628 mg | Sodium |
| 22 g | Fat | 69 mg | Cholesterol |

# Bread Pudding with Raisins

*Makes 16 Servings*

| | |
|---|---|
| ½ | cup sugar |
| ¼ | cup firmly packed brown sugar |
| 1 | teaspoon cinnamon |
| 1 | teaspoon nutmeg |
| 3 | large eggs, lightly beaten |
| 1½ | cups milk substitute |
| 1½ | cups water |
| 2 | tablespoons milk-free margarine, melted |
| 2 | teaspoons vanilla |
| 6 | cups (10 slices) slightly dry white bread (leave crust on), cubed |
| ¾ | cup raisins |

In a large bowl combine the sugars. Add cinnamon and nutmeg and mix well. Reserve 2 tablespoons of this mixture. To the remaining mixture add eggs and mix well. Then stir in milk substitute, water, margarine, and vanilla. Toss the bread cubes with the raisins and add to the liquid mixture. Mix well until all the bread cubes are moistened. Let rest about 15 minutes to absorb the liquid. Transfer the cubes and any extra liquid to a greased 8-inch square baking dish. Sprinkle with reserved cinnamon and sugar mixture. Bake at 325° for about 1 hour or until a knife inserted in the center comes out almost clean.

| Each serving provides: | | | |
|---|---|---|---|
| 149 | Calories | 47 g | Carbohydrate |
| 5 g | Protein | 107 mg | Sodium |
| 5 g | Fat | 103 mg | Cholesterol |

# Cashew Stuffing

*Makes 12 Servings*

| | |
|---|---|
| 1 | cup chopped celery |
| 1 | cup chopped onion |
| ⅓ | cup milk-free margarine |
| 6 | cups fresh breadcrumbs (12 slices) |
| 1 | teaspoon thyme |
| | Salt |
| | Pepper |
| 1 | cup cashew nuts |
| ¼ | cup snipped parsley |

Sauté celery and onion in margarine. Stir in breadcrumbs, thyme, salt and pepper to taste, nuts, and parsley. Place in a 6-cup casserole and bake at 350° about 30 minutes.

---

Each serving provides:

| | | | |
|---|---|---|---|
| 179 | Calories | 17 g | Carbohydrate |
| 4 g | Protein | 182 mg | Sodium |
| 11 g | Fat | .67 mg | Cholesterol |

# Apple Stuffing

*Makes 12 Servings*

| | |
|---|---|
| 1 | loaf dried bread, cut into ½-inch cubes |
| ⅓ | cup milk-free margarine, melted |
| 1 | medium onion, chopped |
| ½ | cup chopped celery |
| ¼ | cup chopped celery leaves |
| 2 | tablespoons chopped parsley |
| ¼ | teaspoon salt |
| ¼ | teaspoon pepper |
| 1 | cup milk substitute |
| 1 | cup water |
| 2 | eggs, slightly beaten |
| 2 | McIntosh apples, pared and chopped (3 cups) |
| ¼ | cup raisins |

Preheat oven to 350°. Grease a 6-cup baking dish. Mix all ingredients together and bake about 45 minutes.

---

| Each serving provides: | | | |
|---|---|---|---|
| 224 | Calories | 31 g | Carbohydrate |
| 5 g | Protein | 356 mg | Sodium |
| 9 g | Fat | 47 mg | Cholesterol |

# Soups

## Cream-of-Celery Soup

*Makes 12 Servings*

¼  cup vegetable oil
4   cups chopped celery with greens
½   cup uncooked rice
6   cups chicken broth
6   cups water
    Salt and pepper

In a large soup pot pour enough oil to cover bottom. Heat until very hot. Add celery and cook until warmed through. Add rice and cook for one minute. Add broth and water and cook until rice is done. Salt and pepper to taste. Let set until room temperature. Purée in blender.

| Each serving provides: | | | |
|---|---|---|---|
| 91 | Calories | 9 g | Carbohydrate |
| 2 g | Protein | 538 mg | Sodium |
| 6 g | Fat | 00 mg | Cholesterol |

# Pottage Jardiniere

*Makes 8 Servings*

2    tablespoons milk-free margarine
2    medium onions, finely chopped
1    quart plus 1 cup chicken broth
2    potatoes, peeled and thinly sliced
2    celery stalks, cut up
1    large carrot, cut up
1    cup fresh green beans, cut in half
1    cup fresh peas
½    cup spinach
1    teaspoon celery salt
½    teaspoon salt
¼    teaspoon pepper
2-3  ounces sherry
     Croutons

In a large soup pot, melt margarine and sauté onions. Add
broth and potatoes. Bring to a boil. Add celery, carrots, beans,
peas, and spinach. Simmer 45 minutes. Add celery salt, salt, and
pepper. Cool soup. Put in a blender to purée. Add sherry. Serve
with croutons floating atop each bowl.

| Each serving provides: | | | |
|---|---|---|---|
| 108 | Calories | 15 g | Carbohydrate |
| 4 g | Protein | 998 mg | Sodium |
| 5 g | Fat | 00 mg | Cholesterol |

# Meatball Soup

*Makes 8 Servings*

| | |
|---|---|
| 1½ | pounds ground beef or veal |
| ½ | cup milk-free bread crumbs |
| 1 | tablespoon parsley flakes |
| 1 | teaspoon salt |
| ½ | teaspoon pepper |
| 3 | tablespoons milk-free margarine |
| 2 | onions, chopped fine |
| 2 | carrots, chopped fine |
| ½ | cup celery, chopped fine |
| 1 | 14-ounce can tomatoes |
| 1 | bay leaf |
| 2 | cups beef broth |
| ¼ | teaspoon basil |

Combine meat, bread crumbs, parsley, salt, and pepper. Form into 1-inch balls. In a large skillet, heat 1 tablespoon milk-free margarine and add meatballs. Brown about 10 minutes. Drain on paper towel. In a large saucepan, heat remaining margarine, and sauté onions, carrots, and celery. Stir in tomatoes, bay leaf, beef broth. Bring to a boil. Add basil and meatballs. Simmer, covered, for about 20 minutes. Remove bay leaf before serving.

| Each serving provides: | | | |
|---|---|---|---|
| 272 | Calories | 11 g | Carbohydrate |
| 16 g | Protein | 721 mg | Sodium |
| 18 g | Fat | 52 mg | Cholesterol |

# Tomato Bisque

### *Makes 4 Servings*

| | |
|---|---|
| 1 | small onion, chopped |
| ¼ | cup green pepper, chopped |
| 1 | tablespoon milk-free margarine |
| 3 | medium tomatoes, peeled and diced |
| ¼ | cup water |
| 1 | cube chicken bouillon |
| ½ | teaspoon dried dill weed |
| | Dash salt |
| 1½ | cups tomato juice |

Sauté onions and pepper in margarine. Add tomatoes, water, bouillon cube, dill, and salt. Cover and simmer for 20 minutes; then let cool. Beat in the blender until thoroughly combined. Add juice and blend. Pour into a pitcher or bowl. Serve hot or cold. Yields about 4 cups.

---

Each serving provides:

| 65 | Calories | 9 g | Carbohydrate |
|---|---|---|---|
| 2 g | Protein | 645 mg | Sodium |
| 3 g | Fat | 00 mg | Cholesterol |

# Potato Soup Base for Chowder

*Makes 2 Servings*

3   medium potatoes, peeled and diced
2   cups chicken bouillon or stock

Add diced potatoes to bouillon or stock and bring to a boil.
Cover and simmer for 25 minutes. Blend on High in a blender
or food processor to liquefy. Yields about 3 cups.

| | Each serving provides: | | |
|---|---|---|---|
| 111 | Calories | 22 g | Carbohydrate |
| 4 g | Protein | 676 mg | Sodium |
| 2 g | Fat | 00 mg | Cholesterol |

# Pacific Chowder

*Makes 2 Servings*

1   cup Potato Soup Base
    Chicken bouillon or stock
1   7-ounce can tuna, drained and flaked

Thin Potato Soup Base with bouillon or stock as desired. Add
flaked tuna, and heat. Yields about 2 cups.

| | Each serving provides: | | |
|---|---|---|---|
| 231 | Calories | 11 g | Carbohydrate |
| 27 g | Protein | 829 mg | Sodium |
| 8 g | Fat | 15 mg | Cholesterol |

# Clam Chowder

*Makes 2 Servings*

1   cup Potato Soup Base
    Clam juice
1   6.5-ounce can clams, drained and rinsed

Thin Potato Soup Base with desired amount of clam juice.
Add clams and heat. Yields about 2 cups.

| | Each serving provides: | | |
|---|---|---|---|
| 115 | Calories | 14 g | Carbohydrate |
| 11 g | Protein | 560 mg | Sodium |
| 2 g | Fat | 36 mg | Cholesterol |

# Seafood Chowder

*Makes 4 Servings*

3   medium potatoes, peeled and diced
2   cups chicken bouillon or stock
1   cup chopped seafood (shrimp, crab meat, clams, tuna)
Salt and pepper to taste

Add diced potatoes to bouillon or stock and bring to a boil.
Cover and simmer for 25 minutes. Liquefy in a blender. Return
to saucepan and thin with hot water if necessary. Add chopped
seafood and season to taste.

| | Each serving provides: | | |
|---|---|---|---|
| 118 | Calories | 16 g | Carbohydrate |
| 10 g | Protein | 586 mg | Sodium |
| 2 g | Fat | 69 mg | Cholesterol |

# Crab Bisque

*Makes 2 Servings*

1    cup Potato Soup Base

¼    cup water

1    cup crab meat, flaked, with cartilage removed

¼    cup white wine

Thin Potato Soup Base with water; add crab meat and wine. Heat and serve. Yields about 2 cups.

---

Each serving provides:

| | | | |
|---|---|---|---|
| 135 | Calories | 11 g | Carbohydrate |
| 18 g | Protein | 556 mg | Sodium |
| 2 g | Fat | 78 mg | Cholesterol |

---

# Cream-of-Vegetable Soup

*Makes 3 Servings*

1    cup puréed vegetables (raw or cooked)

2    cups White Sauce #1

     Water

     Salt and pepper to taste

Combine puréed vegetables with White Sauce, and add enough water to thin adequately. Heat thoroughly and season. Yields about 3 cups.

---

Each serving provides:

| | | | |
|---|---|---|---|
| 157 | Calories | 11 g | Carbohydrate |
| 3 g | Protein | 762 mg | Sodium |
| 11 g | Fat | 91 mg | Cholesterol |

# Vichyssoise

*Makes 4 Servings*

½    cup scallions, chopped, reserve greens
1    tablespoon milk-free margarine
4    cubes chicken bouillon
3    cups boiling water
3    medium potatoes, peeled and diced
½    teaspoon salt
¼    teaspoon white pepper

Brown scallions in margarine and set aside. Prepare bouillon by combining cubes and boiling water. Add potatoes and 2 cups of bouillon to scallions. Add salt and pepper and bring to a boil. Reduce heat; cover and simmer for 25 minutes. Cool and beat in a blender until thoroughly combined. The more you blend, the thicker the soup. Put in a bowl or pitcher and chill overnight. Garnish with chopped scallion greens and serve cold. Yields about 1 quart.

| Each serving provides: | | | |
|---|---|---|---|
| 104 | Calories | 17 g | Carbohydrate |
| 3 g | Protein | 1418 mg | Sodium |
| 3 g | Fat | .59 mg | Cholesterol |

# Cream of Chicken Soup

*Makes 8 Servings*

2  cups chicken stock or bouillon

2  small potatoes, peeled and diced

1  large carrot, peeled and sliced

½  cup celery, chopped

¼  cup celery leaves

   Salt and pepper to taste

Bring stock or bouillon to a boil. Add vegetables, salt, and pepper and return to a boil. Cover and simmer for 25 minutes. Pour into a blender and liquefy. Serve hot. If soup is too thick, use milk substitute or bouillon to thin. Yields about 3 cups.

| Each serving provides: | | | |
|---|---|---|---|
| 94 | Calories | 18 g | Carbohydrate |
| 3 g | Protein | 705 mg | Sodium |
| 1 g | Fat | 00 mg | Cholesterol |

# Gazpacho

*Makes 4 Servings*

½   onion, chopped
½   cucumber, peeled and seeded, chopped
¼   green pepper, chopped
½   garlic clove
5   ripe tomatoes, peeled, seeded, and chopped
1   tablespoon olive oil
1   tablespoon red wine vinegar
1   teaspoon lemon juice
2   dashes tabasco
1   tablespoon minced chives
4   stalks celery with leaves

Place all ingredients except chives and celery in a blender or food processor and purée until smooth. Chill several hours. Sprinkle chives over soup and garnish with celery stalk. Serve cold. Makes 4 1-cup servings.

| Each serving provides: | | | |
|---|---|---|---|
| 75 | Calories | 10 g | Carbohydrate |
| 2 g | Protein | 50 mg | Sodium |
| 4 g | Fat | 00 mg | Cholesterol |

# Salads

## Taco Salad

*Makes 4 Servings*

| | |
|---|---|
| 1 | pound ground beef |
| ¼ | cup chopped onion |
| ¼ | cup chopped green pepper |
| ½ | teaspoon chili powder |
| 4 | prepared taco salad shells |
| 1 | head lettuce, shredded |
| 1 | cup chopped tomatoes |
| 1 | cup chopped black olives |

In a skillet, brown beef with onion, green pepper, and chili powder. Pour off fat. In a taco salad shell layer half full with lettuce. Add meat, then tomatoes and olives. Serve with guacamole or taco sauce.

| | Each serving provides: | | |
|---|---|---|---|
| 531 | Calories | 33 g | Carbohydrate |
| 24 g | Protein | 546 mg | Sodium |
| 34 g | Fat | 69 mg | Cholesterol |

# Spinach Salad

*Makes 4 Servings*

| 1 | pound spinach (rinsed and dried, stems removed) |
|---|---|
| 1 | cup water chestnuts |
| 1 | 11-ounce can mandarin oranges, drained |
| ½ | cup olive or vegetable oil |
| ½ | cup sugar |
| ½ | cup vinegar |
| ½ | cup chili sauce |
| 1 | teaspoon salt |
| 1 | small onion, diced |

Toss together spinach, water chestnuts, and mandarin orange sections in a salad bowl. In a separate bowl, combine remaining ingredients to make dressing. Pour over salad and serve.

Each serving provides:

| 460 | Calories | 55 g | Carbohydrate |
|---|---|---|---|
| 4 g | Protein | 1080 mg | Sodium |
| 27 g | Fat | 00 mg | Cholesterol |

# Caesar Salad

*Makes 4 Servings*

| | |
|---|---|
| 1 | head romaine lettuce, washed and dried |
| 1 | clove garlic |
| 1 | 2-ounce can boneless anchovies |
| ¼ | cup olive or vegetable oil |
| ¼ | teaspoon salt |
| | Dash white pepper |
| 2 | teaspoons Worcestershire sauce |
| 1 | tablespoon lemon juice |
| 2 | coddled eggs |
| | Milk-Free Croutons |

Tear romaine leaves into large pieces and place in a wooden bowl that has been rubbed with garlic. Mash anchovies and combine with oil, salt, pepper, Worcestershire sauce, and lemon juice. Blend well. Pour this on top of romaine leaves. Pour eggs over and toss with two forks. Add croutons and toss again. Serve at once.

| Each serving provides: | | | |
|---|---|---|---|
| 209 | Calories | 5 g | Carbohydrate |
| 9 g | Protein | 661 mg | Sodium |
| 18 g | Fat | 142 mg | Cholesterol |

# Mandarin Salad

*Makes 6 Servings*

1    medium bunch leaf lettuce
1    8-ounce can water chestnuts, drained and sliced
½    pound fresh mushrooms, sliced
2    green onions, sliced on the diagonal
1    6-ounce package frozen pea pods, thawed and well
     drained
     Alfalfa sprouts
     Salted peanuts, coarsely ground


*Dressing*

3    ounces salad oil
1    ounce white wine vinegar
1    tablespoon soy sauce

Tear lettuce into medium-sized pieces and place in a large
salad bowl. Top with water chestnuts, mushrooms, onions, and
pea pods. Just before serving, top with sprouts and peanuts.
Mix oil, vinegar, and soy sauce and pour over salad.

---

|  | Each serving provides: | | |
|---|---|---|---|
| 171 | Calories | 10 g | Carbohydrate |
| 3 g | Protein | 181 mg | Sodium |
| 14 g | Fat | 00 mg | Cholesterol |

# Elegant Salad

*Makes 4 Servings*

1   head romaine lettuce
1   head bibb lettuce
1   tomato, peeled and chopped
1   14-ounce can hearts of palm, drained
1   14-ounce can artichoke hearts, drained
    Lemon-Mustard Dressing

To prepare lettuce, remove leaves one at a time, rinse and drain. Pat dry if necessary. Tear lettuce into large pieces and mix gently. Chop tomato. Cut hearts of palm and artichoke hearts into chunks. For each serving, put some lettuce on the plate, top with vegetables, and sprinkle with chopped tomato. Serve with Lemon-Mustard Dressing.

# Lemon-Mustard Dressing

6     tablespoons vegetable oil
2½    teaspoons fresh lemon juice
1     teaspoon sugar
1     teaspoon salt
½     teaspoon pepper
½     teaspoon Dijon mustard
1     small clove garlic, crushed

Combine these ingredients and shake well. Refrigerate until ready to serve, at least one hour.

| Each serving provides: | | | |
|---|---|---|---|
| 279 | Calories | 19 g | Carbohydrate |
| 7 g | Protein | 621 mg | Sodium |
| 21 g | Fat | 00 mg | Cholesterol |

# Stuffed-Tomato Salad

*Makes 6 Servings*

| | |
|---|---|
| 6 | firm tomatoes |
| ½ | cup cucumber, diced |
| ¼ | cup green pepper, diced |
| ¼ | cup celery, diced |
| ¼ | cup hearts of palm, diced |
| | Salt and pepper to taste |
| 2 | tablespoons olive oil |
| 1 | tablespoon tarragon vinegar |
| | Dill weed |

Rinse and dry tomatoes; slice off tops and discard. Scoop out seeds and pulp into a bowl. Add cucumber, green pepper, celery, and hearts of palm. Salt and pepper to taste. Add oil and vinegar. Mix well, but gently. Fill tomato cups with diced vegetable mixture and top with a sprinkle of dill. Serve very cold.

| Each serving provides: | | | |
|---|---|---|---|
| 70 | Calories | 7 g | Carbohydrate |
| 1 g | Protein | 15 mg | Sodium |
| 5 g | Fat | 00 mg | Cholesterol |

# Louisiana Salad

*Makes 4 Servings*

1   green pepper, sliced thin
1   red pepper, sliced thin
1   yellow pepper, sliced thin
1   package frozen snow peas, thawed
1   head bibb lettuce, torn into medium-sized pieces
1   head Boston lettuce, torn into medium-sized pieces
    Red Onion Dressing

Mix vegetables together and top with dressing to serve.


# Red Onion Dressing

½   cup olive oil
¼   cup red wine vinegar
1   tablespoon chopped red onion
½   teaspoon salt
¼   teaspoon pepper

Combine ingredients. Blend or shake well.

---

Each serving provides:

| 289 | Calories | 10 g | Carbohydrate |
|-----|----------|------|--------------|
| 3 g | Protein | 285 mg | Sodium |
| 28 g | Fat | 00 mg | Cholesterol |

# Summer Fruit Salad

*Makes 6 Servings*

2   cups watermelon chunks
1   cup cantaloupe chunks
1   cup honeydew chunks
1   pint fresh blueberries, rinsed and drained
½   cup coconut
½   cup softened sorbet

Put fruit in a bowl and top with coconut. Cover the bowl and refrigerate for 1-2 hours. Remove the liquid from the bottom of the bowl and mix with sorbet. Toss fruit with sorbet mixture and serve.

| Each serving provides: | | | |
|---|---|---|---|
| 117 | Calories | 21 g | Carbohydrate |
| 1 g | Protein | 13 mg | Sodium |
| 4 g | Fat | 00 mg | Cholesterol |

# Autumn Fruit Salad

*Makes 6 Servings*

2   soft pears, peeled and diced

2   firm bananas, sliced

2   ripe apples, peeled, cored, and cut into chunks

2   naval oranges, peeled and sectioned

1   pink or white grapefruit, peeled and sectioned

1-2 tablespoons mayonnaise

Gently toss the fruit in a chilled bowl. Add enough mayonnaise to moisten. Serve immediately.

| Each serving provides: | | | |
|---|---|---|---|
| 150 | Calories | 32 g | Carbohydrate |
| 1 g | Protein | 20 mg | Sodium |
| 3 g | Fat | 2 mg | Cholesterol |

# Authentic Waldorf Salad

*Makes 4 Servings*

3   cups apple chunks

½   cup walnuts, chopped

½   cup celery, chopped

½   cup raisins

1-2 tablespoons mayonnaise

Blend ingredients, using enough mayonnaise to moisten. Refrigerate, covered, for about an hour before serving.

| Each serving provides: | | | |
|---|---|---|---|
| 239 | Calories | 30 g | Carbohydrate |
| 3 g | Protein | 46 mg | Sodium |
| 14 g | Fat | 3 mg | Cholesterol |

# Four-Bean Salad

*Makes 8 Servings*

| | |
|---|---|
| 1 | 16-ounce can green beans |
| 1 | 16-ounce can wax beans |
| 1 | 16-ounce can garbanzo beans |
| 1 | 16-ounce can kidney beans |
| ½ | cup onion, chopped |
| ½ | cup green pepper, minced |
| ½ | cup vegetable oil |
| ½ | cup vinegar |
| ¾ | cup sugar |
| 1 | teaspoon salt |
| ½ | teaspoon pepper |
| ¼ | teaspoon prepared mustard |

Empty cans of beans into a colander and rinse and drain well. Remove loose skins from garbanzo beans. Place beans in a bowl and add onion and green pepper. To make dressing, mix remaining ingredients, stirring well to dissolve sugar. Pour dressing over beans and refrigerate for several hours before serving. Toss occasionally.

---

Each serving provides:

| | | | |
|---|---|---|---|
| 327 | Calories | 45 g | Carbohydrate |
| 7 g | Protein | 821 mg | Sodium |
| 14 g | Fat | 00 mg | Cholesterol |

# Ambrosia

*Makes 8 Servings*

| | |
|---|---|
| 2-3 | oranges, peeled and sectioned |
| 2 | firm bananas, sliced |
| 1 | cup canned pineapple chunks, drained |
| 1 | cup miniature marshmallows |
| ½ | cup maraschino cherries |
| ¼ | cup cherry juice |
| | Shredded coconut |

Gently toss oranges, bananas, pineapple, marshmallows, and cherries. Add cherry juice and desired amount of coconut. Toss and chill.

---

Each serving provides:

| 114 | Calories | 29 g | Carbohydrate |
|---|---|---|---|
| 1 g | Protein | 3 mg | Sodium |
| .30 g | Fat | .06 mg | Cholesterol |

# Shoepeg Salad

*Makes 8 Servings*

1    16-ounce can white shoepeg corn, drained
1    ounce pimento, drained
¼    cup chopped green pepper
¼    cup chopped green onion
1    celery rib, sliced thinly
¼    cup sugar
¼    cup olive oil
¼    cup vinegar
¼    teaspoon salt

Combine all these ingredients. Toss lightly. Cover tightly and refrigerate overnight. Drain for approximately 30 minutes before serving. Will keep several weeks in the refrigerator.

---

Each serving provides:

| | | | |
|---|---|---|---|
| 133 | Calories | 16 g | Carbohydrate |
| 1 g | Protein | 226 mg | Sodium |
| 7 g | Fat | 00 mg | Cholesterol |

# Confetti Coleslaw

*Makes 8 Servings*

| | |
|---|---|
| 6 | cups shredded green and purple cabbage |
| ½ | cup cider vinegar |
| ¼ | cup vegetable oil |
| 1 | teaspoon dry mustard |
| 1 | teaspoon celery seed |
| 1 | teaspoon salt |
| 3½ | cups water |
| 1 | 6-ounce package lemon gelatin |
| 1 | cup finely shredded carrot |
| ½ | cup thinly sliced radishes |
| ¼ | cup chopped green onion |
| ½ | cup chopped red bell pepper |

Put cabbage in a large bowl. In a small saucepan, stir vinegar,oil, mustard, celery seed, and salt. Bring to a boil over medium heat. Pour over cabbage and let stand 1 hour to flavor. During that time, bring 2 cups water to a boil. Stir in lemon gelatin until completely dissolved. Add 1½ cups cold water. Drain cabbage, reserving liquid. Stir liquid into gelatin. Add carrot, radishes, green onions, and red pepper. Toss to mix. Press cabbage into a 6-cup mold. Pour gelatin liquid over. Cover and refrigerate at least 3 hours or until firm.

| Each serving provides: | | | |
|---|---|---|---|
| 165 | Calories | 25 g | Carbohydrate |
| 3 g | Protein | 359 mg | Sodium |
| 7 g | Fat | 00 mg | Cholesterol |

# Carrot Salad

*Makes 4 Servings*

2    cups grated carrots
½    cup mayonnaise
½    cup raisins
3    teaspoons honey
½    cup drained pineapple chunks

Blend all ingredients. Toss and chill until serving time.

| Each serving provides: | | | |
|---|---|---|---|
| 310 | Calories | 30 g | Carbohydrate |
| 2 g | Protein | 178 mg | Sodium |
| 22 g | Fat | 16 mg | Cholesterol |

# Gazpacho Salad Ring

*Makes 8 Servings*

1    46-ounce can tomato juice
3    envelopes unflavored gelatin
1    clove garlic, crushed
1    teaspoon salt
¼    teaspoon white pepper
2    tablespoons wine vinegar
½    teaspoon Worcestershire sauce
⅛    teaspoon tabasco
½    cup peeled, chopped tomatoes
½    cup diced cucumber
¼    diced green pepper
¼    cup chopped green onion

Pour 2 cups tomato juice into a saucepan and sprinkle with gelatin. Let stand to soften. Heat to boiling and stir to dissolve. Remove from heat and add remaining juice. Add all the remaining ingredients. Pour into an oiled 2-quart ring mold. Chill several hours. Unmold and serve.

| Each serving provides: | | | |
|---|---|---|---|
| 45 | Calories | 9 g | Carbohydrate |
| 4 g | Protein | 916 mg | Sodium |
| .13 g | Fat | 00 mg | Cholesterol |

# Cherry-Wine Mold

*Makes 4 Servings*

| 1 | 1-ounce can pitted bing cherries |
|---|---|
| 1 | cup boiling water |
| 1 | 3-ounce package cherry jello |
| ⅓ | cup red wine |
| ½ | cup chopped nuts |
| 2 | stalks celery, diced fine |
| | Water |

Drain cherries well. Dissolve gelatin in boiling water. Measure cherry juice and wine to make ¾ cup liquid. Add additional water if necessary. Add this liquid to dissolved gelatin. Blend well. Let cool until syrupy. Add cherries, nuts, and celery. Pour into a 1-quart mold. Refrigerate until well set.

| Each serving provides: | | | |
|---|---|---|---|
| 268 | Calories | 42 g | Carbohydrate |
| 5 g | Protein | 91 mg | Sodium |
| 9 g | Fat | 00 mg | Cholesterol |

# Super-Nutritious Vitamin Mold

*Makes 4 Servings*

| | |
|---|---|
| 1 | tablespoon unflavored gelatin |
| ¼ | cup cold water |
| 1 | cup hot orange juice |
| ½ | cup sugar |
| ½ | cup bananas, sliced |
| ½ | cup orange sections, diced |
| ½ | cup carrot, shredded |

Soften gelatin in the cold water. Add hot orange juice and stir until gelatin is dissolved. Stir in sugar. Chill until syrupy; then fold in bananas, oranges, and carrots. Pour into four individual ½-cup molds and chill until firm.

Each serving provides:

| 164 | Calories | 40 g | Carbohydrate |
|---|---|---|---|
| 2 g | Protein | 7 mg | Sodium |
| 0 g | Fat | 00 mg | Cholesterol |

# Cherry-Waldorf Gelatin

*Makes 8 Servings*

| | |
|---|---|
| 1 | 3-ounce package apple gelatin |
| 1 | cup boiling water |
| 1 | cup cold water |
| 1 | 3-ounce package cherry gelatin |
| ⅔ | cup boiling water |
| ⅔ | cup cold water |
| 1½ | teaspoons lemon juice |
| ½ | cup mayonnaise |
| ½ | cup apples, chopped |
| ½ | cup walnuts, chopped |

Dissolve apple gelatin in 1 cup boiling water. Add 1 cup cold water and stir. Pour into a 3-cup mold and refrigerate. Prepare cherry gelatin by dissolving in ⅔ cup boiling water and adding ⅔ cup cold water. Add lemon juice. Refrigerate cherry gelatin until thick and syrupy; then beat in mayonnaise. Fold in apples and walnuts. Set aside. When apple gelatin is almost set, pour cherry mixture on top. Chill until firm. Unmold gelatin onto a serving plate.

| Each serving provides: | | | |
|---|---|---|---|
| 230 | Calories | 43 g | Carbohydrate |
| 6 g | Protein | 293 mg | Sodium |
| 31 g | Fat | 16 mg | Cholesterol |

# Citrus Mold

*Makes 8 Servings*

| | |
|---|---|
| 1 | 3-ounce package orange gelatin |
| 1 | 3-ounce package raspberry gelatin |
| 1⅔ | cups hot orange juice |
| 1⅔ | cups cold grapefruit juice |
| 1½ | cups prepared Rich's Richwhip |
| 2 | naval oranges, sectioned |
| 1 | grapefruit, sectioned |

In a bowl, mix orange and raspberry gelatin crystals. Add hot orange juice and stir until dissolved. Add grapefruit juice and let mixture sit at room temperature. When thick, but not set, beat in milk-free whipping cream. Blend well. Line bottom of a 6-cup circular mold with orange and grapefruit sections. Fill with gelatin mixture and chill until firm. Fruit will rise.

| Each serving provides: | | | |
|---|---|---|---|
| 178 | Calories | 40 g | Carbohydrate |
| 3 g | Protein | 76 mg | Sodium |
| 3 g | Fat | 00 mg | Cholesterol |

# Dressings and Sauces

## Vegetarian Spaghetti Sauce

*Makes 8 Servings*

2      cups sliced zucchini
½      cup sliced fresh mushrooms
½      cup chopped green pepper
½      cup chopped onion
½      teaspoon garlic powder
2      tablespoons olive oil
1      14.5-ounce can peeled tomatoes
1      6-ounce can tomato paste
½      cup water
1      teaspoon salt
½      teaspoon pepper
1      tablespoon parsley flakes
1      teaspoon oregano

In the olive oil, gently sauté zucchini, mushrooms, green pepper, onion, and garlic powder. Add tomatoes, tomato paste, water, and additional spices. Stir to break up tomatoes. Bring the sauce to a boil and continue cooking, uncovered, 20 minutes. Stir occasionally. Serve over pasta, veal, chicken, or beef.

| Each serving provides: | | | |
|---|---|---|---|
| 70 | Calories | 9 g | Carbohydrate |
| 2 g | Protein | 529 mg | Sodium |
| 4 g | Fat | 00 mg | Cholesterol |

# Spaghetti Sauce

*Makes 8 Servings*

| | |
|---|---|
| 2 | medium onions, minced |
| 2 | cloves garlic, minced |
| ¼ | cup olive oil |
| 1½ | pounds ground sirloin |
| 2 | 6-ounce cans tomato paste |
| 2 | cups tomato juice |
| 2 | teaspoons salt |
| ½ | teaspoon pepper |
| 2 | teaspoons sugar |
| ½ | cup red wine |

Brown onions and garlic in oil. Add beef and brown. Pour off fat. Add remaining ingredients and bring to a boil. Cover and simmer for 3 hours. Add wine and simmer another 15 minutes. Yields about 4 cups.

| Each serving provides: | | | |
|---|---|---|---|
| 325 | Calories | 14 g | Carbohydrate |
| 18 g | Protein | 1146 mg | Sodium |
| 23 g | Fat | 53 mg | Cholesterol |

# White Sauce I

*Makes 8 Servings (½ cup per serving)*

2   tablespoons milk-free margarine
2   tablespoons flour
2   cups chicken bouillon
    Salt and white pepper to taste
1   egg yolk

Melt margarine in a saucepan. Add flour, and blend well.
Slowly pour in 1½ cups bouillon, stirring constantly, and add
salt and pepper. When the mixture just boils, blend 2 tablespoons of hot sauce with egg yolk and add this mixture to sauce.
Stir constantly. Add more bouillon if necessary to thin to desired
consistency. Yields about 4 cups.

| Each serving provides: | | | |
|---|---|---|---|
| 98 | Calories | 4 g | Carbohydrate |
| 3 g | Protein | 832 mg | Sodium |
| 8 g | Fat | 68 mg | Cholesterol |

# White Sauce II

*Makes 8 Servings (½ cup per serving)*

2     tablespoons milk-free margarine
2     tablespoons flour
¼     teaspoon salt
¾     cup milk substitute
¼     cup water

Melt margarine in a small pan. Remove from heat; add flour and salt, and stir until smooth. Combine milk substitute and water. Place pan over low heat. Add liquid gradually and stir until thick. Yields about 4 cups.

| Each serving provides: | | | |
|---|---|---|---|
| 126 | Calories | 8 g | Carbohydrate |
| 1 g | Protein | 238 mg | Sodium |
| 10 g | Fat | 00 mg | Cholesterol |

# Rich Brown Gravy

2      tablespoons milk-free margarine
2-3    tablespoons flour
2      cups beef bouillon or broth
½      teaspoon Chinese brown sauce or Kitchen Bouquet

Melt margarine and blend in flour, stirring constantly until brown. Gradually add bouillon until mixture boils and thickens. Cook 3-5 minutes longer. Add brown sauce for color. Strain if necessary. Yields about 3 cups.

| Each serving provides: | | | |
|---|---|---|---|
| 7 | Calories | .35 g | Carbohydrate |
| 13 g | Protein | 380 mg | Sodium |
| .51 g | Fat | 00 mg | Cholesterol |

# Hollandaise Sauce

3      egg yolks
2      tablespoons lemon juice
½      cup milk-free margarine

Beat egg yolks and lemon juice for 2 minutes with an electric mixer. Melt margarine in a saucepan and slowly pour hot margarine into egg mixture, beating at high speed until fluffy. Yields about 1 cup.

Note: Serve with broccoli, asparagus, ham, or eggs.

| Each serving provides: | | | |
|---|---|---|---|
| 63 | Calories | .18 g | Carbohydrate |
| .58 g | Protein | 69 mg | Sodium |
| 7 g | Fat | 51 mg | Cholesterol |

# Chicken Sauce

2   tablespoons milk-free margarine
2   tablespoons flour
2   cups chicken bouillon
    Salt and pepper to taste
1   egg yolk (or substitute)
2   tablespoons sherry

Melt margarine in a saucepan and add flour. Blend well. Slowly pour in 1½ cups bouillon. Add salt and pepper, stirring constantly. When mixture boils, blend 2 tablespoons of hot sauce with egg yolk. Add egg mixture to hot sauce and stir constantly until well blended. Add sherry and cook on low heat, stirring constantly for about 10 minutes. Add more sherry or bouillon if necessary. Yield: 2 cups.

| | Each serving provides: | | |
|---|---|---|---|
| 13 | Calories | .61 g | Carbohydrate |
| .26 g | Protein | 71 mg | Sodium |
| 1 g | Fat | 9 mg | Cholesterol |

# Barbecue Sauce

| 1 | cup vinegar |
|---|---|
| ½ | cup ketchup |
| ¼ | cup Worcestershire sauce |
| 1 | tablespoon vegetable oil |
| 20 | drops tabasco sauce |

Combine all ingredients in a saucepan and bring to a boil. Simmer for 15 minutes. Yields about 1½ cups.

Each serving provides:

| 15 | Calories | 2 g | Carbohydrate |
|---|---|---|---|
| .18 g | Protein | 88 mg | Sodium |
| .56 g | Fat | 00 mg | Cholesterol |

# Hot Apple-Pear Sauce

| 8-10 | McIntosh apples, peeled and cored |
|---|---|
| 2 | pears, peeled and cored |
| 1 | cup water |
| ½ | cup sugar |
| ½ | teaspoon cinnamon |

Slice apples and pears into a saucepan. Add water, sugar, and cinnamon. Simmer until mixture is thoroughly cooked, about 1 hour, adding more water if necessary. Mash with a potato masher and serve. May also be served cold. Add cherry juice for color, if desired. Yields 2 quarts.

Each serving provides:

| 78 | Calories | 20 g | Carbohydrate |
|---|---|---|---|
| .18 g | Protein | .07 mg | Sodium |
| .30 g | Fat | 00 mg | Cholesterol |

# Strawberry Dressing

1     cup hulled strawberries

½     cup confectioners' sugar

1     egg white

Mash strawberries in a bowl. Add sugar and mix. In a separate bowl, beat egg white until stiff. Add egg white to strawberry mixture, beating well. Spoon onto any fruit salad or piece of cake. Yields about 1 cup.

---

Each serving provides:

| 18 | Calories | 4 g | Carbohydrate |
|---|---|---|---|
| .25 g | Protein | 3 mg | Sodium |
| .03 g | Fat | 00 mg | Cholesterol |

---

# Whipped-Topping Dressing

*Makes 8 1-ounce Servings*

1     8-ounce container Rich's Richwhip

½     cup chopped walnuts

Mix whipping cream according to directions. Add nuts and spoon onto fruit salad or slices.

---

Each serving provides:

| 128 | Calories | 6 g | Carbohydrate |
|---|---|---|---|
| 1 g | Protein | 21 mg | Sodium |
| 13 g | Fat | 00 mg | Cholesterol |

# Sour-Creamless
# Green Goddess Dressing

2 cups mayonnaise

2 tablespoons chives, chopped

1 tablespoon parsley flakes

8 anchovy fillets, finely chopped

2 teaspoons lemon juice

Combine ingredients; mix and refrigerate. Yields about 2 cups.

---

Each serving provides:

| | | | |
|---|---|---|---|
| 101 | Calories | .39 g | Carbohydrate |
| .43 g | Protein | 115 mg | Sodium |
| 11 g | Fat | 9 mg | Cholesterol |

# Italian Dressing

1     cup salad oil
¼     cup vinegar
1     teaspoon sugar
½     teaspoon salt
¼     teaspoon pepper
¼     teaspoon celery seed
1     clove garlic, minced

Combine ingredients; mix and refrigerate. Shake well before serving. Yields about 1½ cups.

| Each serving provides: | | | |
|---|---|---|---|
| 82 | Calories | .34 g | Carbohydrate |
| 00 g | Protein | 46 mg | Sodium |
| 9 g | Fat | 00 mg | Cholesterol |

# Meats

## Stir-Fry Beef

*Makes 5 Servings*

3    tablespoons olive oil

3    tablespoons soy sauce, reserve 1 tablespoon

1    pound sirloin, cut into thin strips

6    green onions, cut into 1-inch diagonals

1    6-ounce can sliced water chestnuts

½    cup cold water

2    tablespoons flour

In a large frying pan or wok, heat oil until very hot. Add 2 tablespoons soy sauce and blend. Add sirloin, stir-frying quickly about 1 minute. Toss in green onions and water chestnuts; blend well. In a separate small bowl, blend cold water with 1 tablespoon soy sauce and flour. Mix until all the flour is dissolved. Pour over meat/vegetable mixture. Turn off the heat and let the sauce sit and thicken. Stir mixture continuously. Serve at once.

| Each serving provides: | | | |
|---|---|---|---|
| 390 | Calories | 9 g | Carbohydrate |
| 17 g | Protein | 664 mg | Sodium |
| 32 g | Fat | 65 mg | Cholesterol |

# Mexican Fajitas

*Makes 4 Servings*

10   soft tortillas
3    tablespoons olive oil
6    green onions, cut into 1-inch pieces
1    whole green pepper, seeded and cut into chunks
1    pound skirt steak, or sirloin, cut into thin strips

Prepare:
1    cup chopped tomatoes
1    cup chopped black olives
1    cup guacamole

Wrap tortillas in foil and keep in a warm 275° oven. In a large frying pan, warm oil and brown green onions and green pepper. Add steak and stir-fry quickly. Turn out onto a warm serving dish. Wrap tortillas in a clean towel to keep warm and moist. Each diner assembles his/her own Fajita, which consists of: meat wrapped in a tortilla and topped with tomatoes, olives, and guacamole.

| Each serving provides: | | | |
|---|---|---|---|
| 764 | Calories | 70 g | Carbohydrate |
| 33 g | Protein | 1145 mg | Sodium |
| 40 g | Fat | 59 mg | Cholesterol |

# London Broil

*Makes 6 Servings*

| | |
|---|---|
| 1½ | pounds choice flank steak |
| 1 | cup olive oil |
| 1 | tablespoon vinegar |
| 1 | clove garlic |
| 2 | tablespoons Worcestershire sauce |

Score the flank steak. Place in a shallow pan. Combine the remaining ingredients in a small bowl and pour over meat. Marinate, covered, at room temperature about 2-3 hours. Turn meat several times. Broil steak about 3 inches from the heat, about 5 minutes on each side. (Longer if you want the steak done medium.) Carve in very thin slices across the grain diagonally.

---

Each serving provides:

| 444 | Calories | .47 g | Carbohydrate |
|---|---|---|---|
| 32 g | Protein | 125 mg | Sodium |
| 34 g | Fat | 90 mg | Cholesterol |

# Hungarian Goulash

*Makes 8 Servings*

| | |
|---|---|
| 4 | tablespoons milk-free margarine |
| 1 | tablespoon paprika |
| 2 | tablespoons flour |
| ½ | teaspoon pepper |
| 2 | pounds chuck or round steak, cubed |
| 1 | 6-ounce can tomato paste |
| 1 | clove garlic |
| 1 | package milk-free onion soup mix |
| 2 | cups water |

Melt margarine in a heavy saucepan. Combine paprika, flour, and pepper. Roll meat in seasoned flour and brown lightly in the saucepan. Stir remaining seasoned flour into the pan. Add all the remaining ingredients. Cover and simmer over low heat about 3 hours or until the meat is tender. Serve over wide noodles.

---

Each serving provides:

| 427 | Calories | 9 g | Carbohydrate |
|---|---|---|---|
| 21 g | Protein | 619 mg | Sodium |
| 34 g | Fat | 83 mg | Cholesterol |

# Beef Burgundy

*Makes 8 Servings*

1   small onion, sliced

2   tablespoons milk-free margarine

2   pounds sirloin, sliced thin

1   tablespoon flour

1   teaspoon salt

¼   teaspoon white pepper

2   cups beef broth

1   cup Burgundy wine

1   pound fresh mushrooms

Sauté onion in margarine. Add meat and brown. Add flour. Season with salt and pepper and stir until smooth. Add ½ cup broth and ¾ cup wine. Simmer 3 hours. Add mushrooms and simmer another hour. When mixture needs more liquid, add remaining wine or broth.

| Each serving provides: | | | |
|---|---|---|---|
| 387 | Calories | 2 g | Carbohydrate |
| 20 g | Protein | 570 mg | Sodium |
| 33 g | Fat | 81 mg | Cholesterol |

# Pepper Steak
*Makes 6 Servings*

| | |
|---|---|
| 2 | tablespoons vegetable oil |
| 1 | small onion, sliced |
| 1-2 | pounds round steak, cut into ¼-inch strips |
| 2 | large green peppers, seeded and cut into chunks |
| 3 | tomatoes, cut into wedges |
| 1 | tablespoon soy sauce |
| 2 | tablespoons Worcestershire sauce |

Heat oil in a large skillet and lightly brown onion. Add meat strips and brown on both sides. Add peppers, tomatoes, soy sauce, and Worcestershire sauce. Bring to a boil. Cover and simmer one hour, or until meat is very tender.

---

Each serving provides:

| 343 | Calories | 6 g | Carbohydrate |
|---|---|---|---|
| 23 g | Protein | 290 mg | Sodium |
| 25 g | Fat | 75 mg | Cholesterol |

# Oven Meatballs

*Makes 6 Servings*

| | |
|---|---|
| 1 | cup milk-free bread crumbs |
| 2 | eggs (or substitute), beaten |
| ½ | cup water |
| 1 | tablespoon ketchup |
| 2 | teaspoons salt |
| ½ | teaspoon white pepper |
| ½ | teaspoon paprika |
| 1½ | pounds ground beef (sirloin, for least fat) |

Put bread crumbs in a bowl. Add eggs and water and blend slightly with a fork. Season with ketchup, onion, salt, pepper, and paprika. Add meat and blend well. Roll into 2-inch balls. Bake in a shallow pan for 30 minutes at 350°.

---

| Each serving provides: | | | |
|---|---|---|---|
| 324 | Calories | 13 g | Carbohydrate |
| 22 g | Protein | 957 mg | Sodium |
| 19 g | Fat | 161 mg | Cholesterol |

# Sweet-and-Sour Meatballs

*Makes 6 Servings*

| | |
|---|---|
| 1 | pound ground beef or veal |
| 1 | egg (or substitute), beaten |
| ½ | cup milk-free bread crumbs |
| 1 | teaspoon garlic |
| 1 | teaspoon white pepper |
| 1½ | cups ketchup |
| 1 | cup ginger ale |
| ½ | cup grape jelly |

In a bowl combine the meat, egg, bread crumbs, garlic, and pepper. Add ½ cup ketchup. Blend well. In a saucepan, pour remaining ketchup, ginger ale, and jelly. Stir over low heat until mixture just boils. With wet hands, form 1-inch meatballs and drop into cooking sauce. Cover and simmer for 1 hour.

---

Each serving provides:

| 436 | Calories | 44 g | Carbohydrate |
|---|---|---|---|
| 15 g | Protein | 850 mg | Sodium |
| 21 g | Fat | 110 mg | Cholesterol |

# Better Burgers

*Makes 4 Servings*

½   pound ground beef

½   pound ground veal

1    egg (or substitute), beaten

½   cup milk-free bread crumbs

¼   cup ketchup

1    teaspoon Worcestershire sauce

Salt, pepper, and garlic powder to taste

Mix all ingredients and blend well. Form 4 large burgers and broil, bake, or grill.

### "Who Needs Cheese!" Toppers

Cheese isn't the only way to dress up a burger. Try one of these:

Grilled tomato
Pineapple slices
Spaghetti sauce with extra oregano
Italian sausage slices
Bacon
Thousand Island Dressing
Guacamole
Vidalia onion

| Each serving provides: | | | |
|---|---|---|---|
| 298 | Calories | 14 g | Carbohydrate |
| 24 g | Protein | 355 mg | Sodium |
| 15 g | Fat | 146 mg | Cholesterol |

# Italian Veal

*Makes 4 Servings*

2     tablespoons olive oil
1     clove garlic, minced
½     cup onion, minced
1     pound veal, sliced thin
2     cups tomato sauce
1     teaspoon oregano
¼     teaspoon white pepper

Heat oil in skillet and sauté garlic and onion. Remove and set aside. Sauté veal on both sides until browned. Add tomato sauce, salt, oregano, pepper, onion, and garlic and simmer for 30 minutes. Serve over noodles.

| Each serving provides: | | | |
|---|---|---|---|
| 292 | Calories | 11 g | Carbohydrate |
| 24 g | Protein | 816 mg | Sodium |
| 17 g | Fat | 81 mg | Cholesterol |

# Ground Veal in Acorn Squash

*Makes 6 Servings*

| | |
|---|---|
| 1 | pound ground veal |
| 1 | egg (or substitute), beaten |
| 2 | tablespoons milk-free bread crumbs |
| ½ | cup chopped green pepper |
| 1 | tablespoon minced onion |
| | Salt and pepper to taste |
| 3 | acorn squash |
| 2 | large tomatoes, sliced |

In a bowl, blend veal, egg, bread crumbs, green pepper, and onion. Add salt and pepper. Cut squash in half and scoop out the seeds. Fill each half with meat mixture and top with a tomato slice. Sprinkle with bread crumbs. Arrange on a cookie sheet and cover each squash half with aluminum foil. Bake at 350° for 30 minutes. Uncover and continue baking another 15 minutes, or until squash is soft.

| Each serving provides: | | | |
|---|---|---|---|
| 233 | Calories | 22 g | Carbohydrate |
| 18 g | Protein | 88 mg | Sodium |
| 9 g | Fat | 99 mg | Cholesterol |

# Veal Tidbits

*Makes 4 Servings*

½   pound sliced mushrooms
2   tablespoons olive oil
1   pound veal, sliced thin
    Salt, pepper, and garlic salt to taste
½   cup white wine
2   tablespoons water

Sauté mushrooms in 1 tablespoon oil. Set aside. In another tablespoon oil, sauté veal gently on each side. Line a baking dish with veal, and season with salt, pepper and garlic salt. Spread mushrooms on top. Pour in white wine and water. Bake at 350° for 45 minutes. If veal becomes dry during baking, add a little water.

| Each serving provides: | | | |
|---|---|---|---|
| 262 | Calories | 3 g | Carbohydrate |
| 23 g | Protein | 81 mg | Sodium |
| 17 g | Fat | 81 mg | Cholesterol |

# Veal-and-Rice Rhapsody

*Makes 8 Servings*

| | |
|---|---|
| 2 | tablespoons flour |
| 1 | teaspoon salt |
| 1½ | pounds cubed veal |
| 3 | tablespoons olive oil |
| 3 | cups water |
| ¼ | cup white wine |
| 1 | 6-ounce package seasoned long grain and wild rice |
| 1 | cup celery, thinly sliced |
| 1 | cup fresh mushrooms, sliced |
| ½ | cup green onions, chopped |

Combine flour and salt. Dredge veal and brown in oil. Pour off the drippings. Add ½ cup water and wine. Cover tightly and simmer 30 minutes. Stir in remaining 2½ cups water, rice, and vegetables. Continue cooking, covered, until the veal and rice are done and all the water is absorbed, about 30 minutes.

| Each serving provides: | | | |
|---|---|---|---|
| 279 | Calories | 18 g | Carbohydrate |
| 20 g | Protein | 662 mg | Sodium |
| 14 g | Fat | 61 mg | Cholesterol |

# Low-Fat Moussaka

*Makes 8 Servings*

| | |
|---|---|
| 1½ | pounds lean ground lamb or ground turkey |
| 2 | onions, diced |
| 4 | tomatoes, chopped fine |
| 3 | tablespoons parsley |
| ½ | teaspoon cinnamon |
| ½ | teaspoon nutmeg |
| ¼ | teaspoon pepper |
| 1 | cup water |
| 3 | tablespoons tomato paste |
| 1 | large eggplant |
| ½ | cup milk-free bread crumbs |
| 2 | tablespoons wheat germ |

Cook meat in a large non-stick skillet, breaking the meat apart with a fork as it cooks. Pour off excess fat. Add onions, tomatoes, parsley, cinnamon, nutmeg, and pepper. Combine water and tomato paste. Add to meat mixture. Cover and simmer for 20 minutes. Peel and slice eggplant into thin slices, about ½ inch. Pour some of the meat/sauce mixture into an 8 × 12-inch baking pan. Arrange a layer of eggplant slices side by side. Cover with more sauce. Continue to fill the pan with layers of eggplant and thin layers of sauce, ending with layer of sauce. Sprinkle with bread crumbs and wheat germ. Bake at 350° for 1 hour.

---

| Each serving provides: | | | |
|---|---|---|---|
| 200 | Calories | 15 g | Carbohydrate |
| 19 g | Protein | 158 mg | Sodium |
| 8 g | Fat | 60 mg | Cholesterol |

# Poultry and Pasta

## Danish Chicken

*Makes 4 Servings*

1  broiler/fryer, cut up, about 3 pounds
3  tablespoons olive oil
   Salt and pepper
3  tablespoons Dijon mustard
2  tablespoons dry white wine
6  tablespoons milk-free bread crumbs

Preheat the broiler. Brush chicken pieces with oil and sprinkle with salt and pepper. Broil chicken about 5 inches from the heat for 5 minutes. Turn and broil 5 minutes more. While chicken is cooking, combine mustard and wine. Remove chicken from the broiler and coat one side with ½ the mustard mixture and 3 tablespoons bread crumbs. Broil 1 minute until browned. Turn and repeat. Remove form the broiler. Set oven at 350°. Bake the chicken 15 minutes more.

| | Each serving provides: | | |
|---|---|---|---|
| 470 | Calories | 8 g | Carbohydrate |
| 42 g | Protein | 529 mg | Sodium |
| 28 g | Fat | 132 mg | Cholesterol |

# Arroz con Pollo

*Makes 4 Servings*

| | |
|---|---|
| 1 | fryer chicken, cut into pieces |
| 1 | large onion, chopped |
| 1 | tablespoon garlic, crushed |
| ½ | cup olive oil |
| 1 | 8-ounce can whole tomatoes |
| 1½ | quarts water or chicken broth |
| 1 | bay leaf |
| 1 | pound long-grain rice |
| 1 | green pepper, chopped |
| ½ | cup sherry |
| 1 | cup small peas |
| 1 | small jar chopped pimento |

Sauté chicken in oil with onion and garlic until lightly browned. Add tomatoes and water or broth and bring to a boil. Add bay leaf, salt, rice, and green pepper. Stir thoroughly and place in a casserole. Bake at 350° for about 25 minutes. Just before serving, stir in sherry, peas, and pimento.

---

Each serving provides:

| 1238 | Calories | 109 g | Carbohydrate |
|---|---|---|---|
| 54 g | Protein | 130 mg | Sodium |
| 63 g | Fat | 174 mg | Cholesterol |

# Spicy Buffalo Wings

*Makes 12 Servings*

2    pounds chicken wings
1    12-ounce jar apricot preserves
1    package milk-free onion soup mix
1    8-ounce bottle Russian dressing
1    teaspoon garlic powder
½    teaspoon ground ginger

Preheat oven to 350°. Clip ends of wings and discard or save to use in soup. Rinse chicken in cold water and pat dry. Combine remaining ingredients and blend well. Spoon over wings. Bake 60 minutes, uncovered, until all the liquid is gone.

| | Each serving provides: | | |
|---|---|---|---|
| 281 | Calories | 24 g | Carbohydrate |
| 9 g | Protein | 417 mg | Sodium |
| 17 g | Fat | 31 mg | Cholesterol |

# Sesame Chicken

*Makes 4 Servings*

| | |
|---|---|
| 1 | chicken fryer, cut up |
| 1 | cup sesame crackers, crushed |
| 1 | teaspoon garlic salt |
| ½ | teaspoon pepper |
| ⅔ | cup milk-free margarine |
| 1 | tablespoon lemon juice |

Rinse chicken in cold water and set aside to dry. Combine crushed crackers with spices. Melt margarine. Dip chicken pieces in margarine, then into crumbs. Place skin side up in a baking dish and sprinkle with remaining crumbs. Sprinkle each piece with a few drops of lemon juice. Bake at 350° about 60 minutes or until chicken is tender.

---

Each serving provides:

| 720 | Calories | 12 g | Carbohydrate |
|---|---|---|---|
| 43 g | Protein | 1128 mg | Sodium |
| 54 g | Fat | 131 mg | Cholesterol |

# Chicken Kiev

*Makes 6 Servings*

¾   cup softened milk-free margarine
1    tablespoon chopped parsley
2    tablespoons finely cut chives
½    teaspoon salt
¼    teaspoon pepper
6    whole boned and skinned chicken breasts
1    egg
2    tablespoons cold water
     Flour
⅔    cup milk-free bread crumbs
¼    cup milk-free margarine

Mix softened margarine with parsley, chives, salt, and pepper. Shape into 6 sticks and freeze until firm. Place chicken breast between 2 pieces of waxed paper and pound with a mallet until about ¼-inch thickness. Place a stick of herbed margarine on each breast. Roll and close edges with a toothpick. Sprinkle lighly with salt and pepper. Heat oven to 400°. Beat egg with water in a flat dish. Dredge breasts with flour, dip in egg mixture, and roll in bread crumbs. Heat margarine in skillet over medium heat. Sauté breasts until golden brown on both sides. Place chicken in a shallow baking pan and bake 15-20 minutes until tender.

| Each serving provides: | | | |
|---|---|---|---|
| 607 | Calories | 15 g | Carbohydrate |
| 56 g | Protein | 781 mg | Sodium |
| 35 g | Fat | 178 mg | Cholesterol |

# Chinese Chicken Crêpes

*Makes 6 Servings*

1     cup chicken, cooked and finely chopped
½    cup mushrooms, chopped
2     tablespoons green pepper, chopped
1     tablespoon onion, chopped
2     eggs (or substitute), beaten
½    teaspoon salt
¼    teaspoon pepper
      Olive or vegetable oil
18   small crêpes
Sweet and Sour Sauce

Combine chicken, mushrooms, green pepper, and onion. Add eggs to chicken mixture; then mix in salt and pepper. Put 1½ tablespoons of this chicken mixture on cooked side of each crêpe. Fold in sides and roll up. Place filled crêpes on an ungreased cookie sheet. Brush with oil. Bake at 400° for 15-20 minutes, or until browned. Top with sauce.

# Sweet and Sour Sauce

½   cup chili sauce

½   cup grape jelly

2   tablespoons lemon juice

½   cup soy sauce

Put all ingredients in a small saucepan and stir to mix. Bring to a boil; then lower the heat and simmer for 15 minutes.

| Each serving provides: | | | |
|---|---|---|---|
| 443 | Calories | 51 g | Carbohydrate |
| 17 g | Protein | 2375 mg | Sodium |
| 19 g | Fat | 249 mg | Cholesterol |

# Lemon-Garlic Chicken

*Makes 2 Servings*

4   boned and skinned chicken breast halves
1   clove garlic, crushed
    Juice of 1 lemon
2   tablespoons vegetable or olive oil
    Thyme to taste
    Fresh-ground pepper to taste

Put all ingredients in a bowl. Toss, cover, and refrigerate for at least 2 hours. Remove chicken from marinade and pat dry with paper towel. Grill or broil.

---

Each serving provides:

| 156 | Calories | .44 g | Carbohydrate |
|---|---|---|---|
| 26 g | Protein | 74 mg | Sodium |
| 5 g | Fat | 66 mg | Cholesterol |

# Chicken à L'Orange

*Makes 8 Servings*

1      egg (or substitute), slightly beaten
¼      cup orange juice
1      cup milk-free bread crumbs
1      teaspoon paprika
1      teaspoon salt
1      tablespoon grated orange peel
2-3    pounds fryer chicken, rinsed, dried, and cut up

Combine egg and orange juice. Beat well. Combine bread crumbs, paprika, salt, and orange peel. Dip chicken in egg mixture, then into bread crumb mixture. Bake covered at 375° for 30 minutes. Uncover and bake another 15 minutes.

| Each serving provides: | | | |
|---|---|---|---|
| 214 | Calories | 11 g | Carbohydrate |
| 20 g | Protein | 427 mg | Sodium |
| 10 g | Fat | 90 mg | Cholesterol |

# Chicken Divan

*Makes 8 Servings*

1   10-ounce package frozen broccoli or ½ pound fresh
    broccoli
    Chicken Sauce (page 144)
8   portions boned and skinned cooked chicken breast
    Milk-free bread crumbs

Steam broccoli. Prepare chicken sauce. Arrange broccoli in an
8 × 11-inch casserole dish and pour half of the chicken sauce
over it. Cover with chicken portions. Pour remaining sauce
over chicken and top with a heavy sprinkling of bread crumbs.
Bake, uncovered, at 375° for 30 minutes.

| Each serving provides: | | | |
|---|---|---|---|
| 225 | Calories | 9 g | Carbohydrate |
| 29 g | Protein | 403 mg | Sodium |
| 7 g | Fat | 107 mg | Cholesterol |

# Broiled Chicken

*Makes 8 Servings (1 per serving)*

2-3   pounds broiler or fryer chicken, rinsed, dried, and cut
      up

½     cup soy sauce

¼     cup Worcestershire sauce

2     pinches crushed rosemary

Put chicken pieces in broiler pan, skin side down, leaving
some room around each. In a small bowl, mix together soy
sauce, Worcestershire sauce, and rosemary. Drizzle half the
sauce over chicken and broil. Turn pieces over and drizzle
remainder of sauce on the other side. Total broiling time is about
40 minutes.

| | Each serving provides: | | |
|---|---|---|---|
| 154 | Calories | 1 g | Carbohydrate |
| 18 g | Protein | 339 mg | Sodium |
| 9 g | Fat | 55 mg | Cholesterol |

# Oven-Fried Chicken

*Makes 8 Servings*

2-3  pounds fryer chicken, cut up
2    cups milk-free bread crumbs
½    teaspoon garlic salt
1    teaspoon salt
½    teaspoon pepper
     Milk-free margarine

Rinse chicken in cold water. Do not dry. Roll in bread crumbs. Place in a baking pan. Mix spices together and shake evenly over chicken. Dot each piece with margarine. Bake, uncovered, without turning, at 375° for about 1 hour.

|  | Each serving provides: |  |  |
|---|---|---|---|
| 225 | Calories | 10 g | Carbohydrate |
| 19 g | Protein | 567 mg | Sodium |
| 12 g | Fat | 56 mg | Cholesterol |

# Chicken Marsala

*Makes 8 Servings (1 per serving)*

3   tablespoons safflower oil
4   whole skinned and boned chicken breasts
    Salt
    Garlic Powder
    Pepper
1   tablespoon milk-free margarine
1   tablespoon flour
½   cup chicken broth
½   cup Marsala wine
1   tablespoon milk substitute
3   medium zucchini, sliced
2   medium tomatoes, cut into 1-inch cubes
½   teaspoon dried basil

In a large skillet, heat 2 tablespoons oil. Sprinkle chicken with salt, garlic powder, and pepper. Sauté chicken until nicely browned. Reduce heat and cook until tender. Remove chicken from the skillet and keep warm in a 250° oven. In the skillet, melt margarine and flour. Cook 30 seconds, stirring constantly to scrape brown particles from the skillet. Reduce heat and cook 5 minutes. Stir in broth, wine, and milk substitute. Spoon this mixture over chicken. Keep warm. In the skillet, heat remaining oil and cook zucchini about 2 minutes. Add tomatoes and chopped basil; blend well. Cook and stir about 2 minutes. Spoon over chicken and serve.

| Each serving provides: | | | |
|---|---|---|---|
| 212 | Calories | 6 g | Carbohydrate |
| 28 g | Protein | 161 mg | Sodium |
| 9 g | Fat | 66 mg | Cholesterol |

# Chinese Chicken Salad

*Makes 4 Servings*

| | |
|---|---|
| 1 | pound boned and skinned chicken breast, cooked |
| 2 | ounces cellophane noodles |
| | Oil |
| 1 | small head of lettuce, cut into strips |
| 4 | stalks green onion, chopped |
| 2 | tablespoons slivered almonds |
| 2 | tablespoons sesame seeds |

Shred chicken meat. Cook the cellophane threads in hot oil a few at a time. Drain on paper towel. Toast almonds and sesame seeds in skillet without oil. Arrange the lettuce in a salad bowl. Top with cellophane noodles, chicken, onion, almonds, and sesame seeds. Pour on the dressing and toss.

# Dressing

| | |
|---|---|
| 2 | tablespoons sugar |
| 1 | teaspoon salt |
| ½ | teaspoon black pepper |
| ¼ | cup oil |
| 3 | tablespoons vinegar |

Blend all ingredients in a bowl.

---

Each serving provides:

| | | | |
|---|---|---|---|
| 352 | Calories | 25 g | Carbohydrate |
| 29 g | Protein | 635 mg | Sodium |
| 27 g | Fat | 66 mg | Cholesterol |

# Oriental Chicken

*Makes 4 Servings*

| | |
|---|---|
| 4 | boned and skinned chicken breasts, cut into 1-inch cubes |
| 1 | tablespoon soy sauce |
| 1 | tablespoon sherry |
| 1 | teaspoon cornstarch |
| 3 | tablespoons vegetable or olive oil |
| 1 | 8-ounce can sliced water chestnuts |
| ½ | pound fresh mushrooms, wiped, and sliced |
| 1 | package frozen pea pods |
| 2 | tablespoons hoisin sauce (or combine ¼ cup ketchup and 2 tablespoons maple syrup) |
| ¼ | cup slivered almonds |
| 1 | tablespoon finely chopped chives |

Mix together soy sauce, sherry, and cornstarch. Marinate chicken cubes in this mixture for 30 minutes. Heat 1 tablespoon oil in heavy skillet or wok. Stir-fry water chestnuts, pea pods, and mushrooms. Remove and set aside. Heat remaining oil. Add marinated chicken and stir-fry until meat is opaque. Add vegetable mixture and hoisin sauce to chicken. Cook for 1 minute longer. Top with nuts and chives.

| Each serving provides: | | | |
|---|---|---|---|
| 355 | Calories | 20 g | Carbohydrate |
| 32 g | Protein | 597 mg | Sodium |
| 17 g | Fat | 66 mg | Cholesterol |

# Grandma's Turkey

|   | Fresh or frozen (and thawed) turkey |
|---|---|
| 2 | large white onion |
| 6 | stalks celery |
| 6 | peeled carrots |
|   | A handful of fresh parsley |
|   | Milk-free margarine, softened |
|   | Salt |
|   | Pepper |
|   | Paprika |
|   | Garlic powder |
| 3 | chicken bouillon cubes |

Prepare turkey by washing well inside and out. Pat dry. Remove giblets and neck. Rinse and let dry on paper towel. Place turkey in a roasting pan, and salt the cavity generously. Put 1 onion, 3 stalks celery, 3 carrots, and the parsley in the cavity. With the remaining spices, make a mixture with the softened margarine and spread all over the turkey with your hands. Fill the pan with about 1 inch of water. Around the sides place the remaining vegetables, turkey parts, and bouillon cubes. Cook turkey gently at 325°, *without covering*, allowing for about 25 minutes a pound. Baste every 30 minutes. Let set for at least 30 minutes to an hour before serving.

---

Each serving provides (light meat):

| 153 | Calories | 00 g | Carbohydrate |
|---|---|---|---|
| 30 g | Protein | 67 mg | Sodium |
| 3 g | Fat | 68 mg | Cholesterol |

| Each serving provides (dark meat): | | | |
|---|---|---|---|
| 184 | Calories | 00 g | Carbohydrate |
| 28 g | Protein | 81 mg | Sodium |
| 7 g | Fat | 87 mg | Cholesterol |

# Turkey Salad

*Makes 8 Servings (½ cup per serving)*

3   cups turkey, cooked and diced
½   pound cashew nuts
1   pound green grapes, seedless
    Mayonnaise
    Salt and pepper
    Lettuce

Toss turkey, cashews, and grapes together with enough mayonnaise to make a light, creamy consistency. Season with salt and pepper. Serve on a bed of lettuce.

| Each serving provides: | | | |
|---|---|---|---|
| 390 | Calories | 20 g | Carbohydrate |
| 21 g | Protein | 123 mg | Sodium |
| 27 g | Fat | 49 mg | Cholesterol |

# Turkey Burgers

*Makes 4 Servings*

| | |
|---|---|
| 2 | cups chopped cooked turkey |
| 1 | egg, slightly beaten |
| ½ | cup mayonnaise |
| ½ | cup diced celery |
| ¼ | cup milk-free bread crumbs |
| 2 | tablespoons chopped onion |
| 2 | tablespoons finely chopped blanched almonds |
| ¼ | teaspoon salt |
| ¼ | teaspoon pepper |
| 1 | tablespoon milk-free margarine |
| | Bread crumbs for coating |

Mix together all ingredients except margarine. Chill well. Shape into 6 patties and roll in bread crumbs. Melt margarine in skillet over medium heat. Cook patties about 10 minutes or until evenly browned on both sides.

---

Each serving provides:

| | | | |
|---|---|---|---|
| 464 | Calories | 16 g | Carbohydrate |
| 26 g | Protein | 546 mg | Sodium |
| 33 g | Fat | 140 mg | Cholesterol |

# Turkey à La King

*Makes 4 Servings*

2    cups cooked turkey, diced
1    3-ounce can sliced mushrooms
½    cup chopped green pepper
½    cup frozen or fresh peas
¼    cup pimento, chopped
    White Sauce #1 (page 141)

Combine all ingredients and simmer for 20-30 minutes, stirring occasionally. To serve, pour over toast points or into patty shells.

| Each serving provides: | | | |
|---|---|---|---|
| 239 | Calories | 8 g | Carbohydrate |
| 24 g | Protein | 731 mg | Sodium |
| 12 g | Fat | 122 mg | Cholesterol |

# Gingered Duck

*Makes 4 Servings*

2   skinned and boned whole duck breasts
6   tablespoons ginger preserves
6   tablespoons orange juice
1   tablespoon lemon juice
1   tablespoon grated orange rind
    Vegetable oil

Rinse duck breasts in cold water and set aside. Spray broiler pan with a non-stick coating. In a small saucepan, combine preserves, juices, and rind. Simmer gently. Brush meat with oil; broil, approximately 3-4 minutes on each side. Remove, slice in thin strips, and serve with sauce.

| | Each serving provides: | | |
|---|---|---|---|
| 312 | Calories | 24 g | Carbohydrate |
| 26 g | Protein | 110 mg | Sodium |
| 12 g | Fat | 109 mg | Cholesterol |

# Pasta Florentine

*Makes 4 Servings*

| | |
|---|---|
| 1 | 8-ounce package spaghetti, cooked and drained |
| 2 | 10-ounce packages frozen chopped spinach, thawed and squeezed dry |
| ½ | cup chopped onion |
| 2 | eggs, well beaten |
| 4 | tablespoons milk-free margarine, melted |
| 1 | 4-ounce jar pimento |
| 5 | ounces fresh mushrooms |
| 2 | tablespoons milk-free margarine |
| 1 | 15.5-ounce jar prepared spaghetti sauce |

To cooked spaghetti add spinach, onion, eggs, melted margarine, and pimento. Blend well. Spray a ring mold with nonstick coating. Press pasta into the mold. Place the mold in a pan of water and bake at 375° about 25 minutes. Let stand 5 minutes before unmolding. While pasta is baking, prepare sauce. Sauté mushrooms in margarine. Add prepared spaghetti sauce, blend, and cook till hot. Serve with sauce in the center of the pasta ring.

---

Each serving provides:

| | | | |
|---|---|---|---|
| 579 | Calories | 71 g | Carbohydrate |
| 18 g | Protein | 895 mg | Sodium |
| 27 g | Fat | 137 mg | Cholesterol |

# Lasagne

*Makes 8 Servings*

4   cups spaghetti sauce
1   16-ounce box lasagne
2   cups milk-free bread crumbs

Bring spaghetti sauce to a boil, remove from heat, and set aside. In a large pot, cook lasagne according to directions on box. Line a 9 × 13-inch glass baking dish or large lasagne pan with half of the lasagne and spread half of the sauce over pasta. Top with half the bread crumbs. Layer on remaining lasagne, sauce, and bread crumbs. Cover with aluminum foil; bake at 350° for 20 minutes. Uncover and continue baking for an additional 20 minutes.

Note: If you can eat Formagg lactose-free cheese products, layer over bread crumbs with a combination Mozzarella and Romano mix.

|  | Each serving provides: |  |  |
|---|---|---|---|
| 632 | Calories | 75 g | Carbohydrate |
| 28 g | Protein | 1331 mg | Sodium |
| 25 g | Fat | 55 mg | Cholesterol |

# Spinach Lasagne

*Makes 8 Servings*

1   16-ounce box lasagne
4   cups spaghetti sauce
3   egg whites
1   teaspoon garlic powder
1   teaspoon oregano
3   tablespoons chopped parsley
2   boxes frozen spinach (thawed)
2   cups milk-free bread crumbs

Prepare lasagne according to directions on box. Rinse with cold water and set aside to drain. Prepare spaghetti sauce and set aside. Beat egg whites until frothy. Combine with garlic powder, oregano, parsley, and spinach. Line a 9 × 13-inch glass pan or a large lasagne pan with a layer of pasta. Top with a generous layer of spaghetti sauce, then spinach mixture, then bread crumbs. Repeat these layers. Bake uncovered at 350° for 30-40 minutes.

| Each serving provides: | | | |
|---|---|---|---|
| 657 | Calories | 78 g | Carbohydrate |
| 31 g | Protein | 1403 mg | Sodium |
| 25 g | Fat | 55 mg | Cholesterol |

# Cold Chicken and Pasta

*Makes 8 Servings*

| | |
|---|---|
| 4-5 | whole boned chicken breasts |
| | Water |
| | Chicken bouillon |
| 1 | 16-ounce box vermicelli |
| 2 | tablespoons white wine vinegar |
| 2 | cloves garlic, crushed |
| ½ | cup olive oil |
| 2 | teaspoons salt |
| 2 | 8.5-ounce jars artichoke hearts |
| 1 | 6-ounce can black olives |
| ½ | pound cherry tomatoes |
| 1 | cup mayonnaise |
| 2 | teaspoons Dijon mustard |

Place chicken breasts in a large pot and add a mixture of half water, half bouillon, enough to cover chicken. Bring to a boil and cook for 30 minutes. Pour off broth. Cool, skin, and cube the chicken; cover and refrigerate. Cook vermicelli according to directions on the box; drain and set aside. Mix together vinegar, garlic, oil, and salt. Toss vermicelli with this mixture and chill thoroughly. Drain artichoke hearts and olives. Slice olives. Rinse tomatoes and remove stems. Add the chicken cubes to the vermicelli and blend in mayonnaise and mustard. Add olives and artichokes. Garnish with cherry tomatoes.

| Each serving provides: | | | |
|---|---|---|---|
| 757 | Calories | 51 g | Carbohydrate |
| 36 g | Protein | 1322 mg | Sodium |
| 46 g | Fat | 82 mg | Cholesterol |

# Fish and Seafood

## Grilled Salmon Steaks with Pineapple Sauce

*Makes 4 Servings*

4 firm salmon steaks, washed in cold water
  Salt and pepper to taste
  Lemon juice

Season salmon steaks with salt, pepper, and lemon juice. Grill on barbecue or in broiler. Serve with Pineapple-Mustard Sauce.

## Pineapple-Mustard Sauce

1 12-ounce can unsweetened pineapple
1 tablespoon Dijon mustard

In a blender, purée pineapple (drained) and add mustard. Blend well and keep cold until salmon steaks are ready to serve.

| Each serving provides: | | | |
|---|---|---|---|
| 298 | Calories | 14 g | Carbohydrate |
| 34 g | Protein | 189 mg | Sodium |
| 11 g | Fat | 94 mg | Cholesterol |

# Salmon Soufflé

*Makes 6 Servings*

| | |
|---|---|
| 3 | carrots |
| 1 | small onion |
| 3 | eggs |
| 1 | 15.5-ounce can red salmon, drained |
| ½ | teaspoon savory |
| ½ | cup milk substitute |
| ½ | cup milk-free bread crumbs |
| ¼ | cup milk-free margarine |

Grate carrots and onion. In a large bowl, beat eggs very well. Add salmon, savory, milk substitute, and bread crumbs. Blend well. Melt margarine and pour into a loaf pan. Combine salmon mixture and vegetables. Press into the loaf pan and bake at 350°, uncovered, 45-55 minutes.

---

Each serving provides:

| 276 | Calories | 13 g | Carbohydrate |
|---|---|---|---|
| 17 g | Protein | 534 mg | Sodium |
| 17 g | Fat | 164 mg | Cholesterol |

# Salmon Croquettes

*Makes 6 Servings*

| | |
|---|---|
| 1 | 15.5-ounce can salmon |
| 1 | egg, slightly beaten |
| ½ | cup chopped Bermuda onion |
| ½ | cup finely chopped green pepper |
| ½ | cup milk-free bread crumbs |
| 1 | teaspoon lemon |
| | Ground black pepper to taste |
| | Vegetable oil or milk-free margarine |

Drain salmon and flake. Crush bones well. Mix with remaining ingredients. Form into small patties. Sauté gently in a small amount of vegetable oil or milk-free margarine. Turn until nicely browned on both sides.

---

Each serving provides:

| 184 | Calories | 8 g | Carbohydrate |
|---|---|---|---|
| 14 g | Protein | 394 mg | Sodium |
| 10 g | Fat | 72 mg | Cholesterol |

# Fillet of Sole in Wine Sauce

*Makes 4 Servings*

1    pound sole fillets
1    cup milk-free bread crumbs
1    tablespoon minced onion
2    tablespoons minced green pepper
2    small tomatoes, chopped fine
½    cup white wine
     Salt and pepper to taste
1    tablespoon flour
     Cold water
2    tablespoons milk-free margarine

Grease a 7½ × 10½-inch baking pan with milk-free margarine. Pour half the bread crumbs and spread along the bottom. Top with onion, green pepper, and tomatoes. Gently place the fish on top and pour on the wine. Season to taste with salt and pepper. Bake at 375° for 20 minutes. Remove the liquid and pour into a small saucepot. Make a paste out of the flour and cold water and add this to the saucepot, cooking gently. Add the milk-free margarine and continue to cook gently until the mixture is thick. Pour sauce over the fish and sprinkle with remaining bread crumbs. Return to oven to brown, about 5 minutes.

| Each serving provides: | | | |
|---|---|---|---|
| 272 | Calories | 23 g | Carbohydrate |
| 25 g | Protein | 348 mg | Sodium |
| 8 g | Fat | 56 mg | Cholesterol |

# Red Snapper Packages

*Makes 4 Servings*

Aluminum foil

4 fillets red snapper (about 6 ounces each), fresh
or frozen

Salt and pepper

½   pound fresh pea pods

2   carrots, cut into thin strips

1   cup fresh mushrooms, cut in half

8   slices lemon

Cut foil into rectangles large enough to wrap around the fish.
Salt and pepper fillets. Lay each fillet in the middle of the foil.
On top of each piece of fish, put some pea pods, some carrot
strips, some mushrooms, and 2 slices of lemon. Wrap the foil
around the fish and vegetables, sealing tightly and tucking the
ends under. Place on a baking sheet and bake in a preheated oven
at 400° about 15 minutes.

| | Each serving provides: | | |
|---|---|---|---|
| 219 | Calories | 12 g | Carbohydrate |
| 38 g | Protein | 125 mg | Sodium |
| 3 g | Fat | 63 mg | Cholesterol |

# Baked Gefilte Fish

*Makes 8 Servings*

2   pounds ground whitefish
2   onions, grated
1   carrot, grated
1   teaspoon vegetable oil
¼   teaspoon salt
¼   teaspoon pepper
½   cup milk-free bread crumbs
2   well-beaten eggs
½   cup cold water
1   green pepper, sliced into rings (remove seeds)

To ground fish add onions, carrot, oil, salt, pepper, and bread crumbs. Beat in eggs and water. Mix well. Place green pepper rings on the bottom of a well-oiled loaf pan. Press in fish mixture. Bake at 325° uncovered about 1 hour. Unmold on a platter. Slice to serve.

| Each serving provides: | | | |
|---|---|---|---|
| 286 | Calories | 10 g | Carbohydrate |
| 32 g | Protein | 257 mg | Sodium |
| 12 g | Fat | 183 mg | Cholesterol |

# French Fillets

*Makes 4 Servings*

8   skinless, boneless fillets of flounder
    Salt and pepper to taste
1   egg
2   tablespoons water
¼   cup flour
3   tablespoons olive oil
3   tablespoons milk-free margarine
2   tablespoons chopped cashews
1   tablespoon lemon juice
1   tablespoon parsley flakes

Salt and pepper fillets as desired. In a shallow dish, beat the egg with salt, pepper, and water. In another shallow dish, spread out the flour. Dip each fillet in flour, then in egg mixture to coat well on all sides. Heat about 2 tablespoons oil in a skillet, using more if necessary. Place the fish in a single layer and cook on medium heat until golden brown on each side. Transfer the fish to a warm platter. Wipe the skillet and add the margarine. When melted, add the nuts and lemon juice. Cook until the nuts are nicely toasted. Pour this sauce over the fish and top with parsley.

| Each serving provides: | | | |
|---|---|---|---|
| 395 | Calories | 8 g | Carbohydrate |
| 35 g | Protein | 257 mg | Sodium |
| 24 g | Fat | 150 mg | Cholesterol |

# Stuffed Fillet of Sole

*Makes 4 Servings*

½  cup milk-free margarine
¼  cup onion, chopped
¼  cup almonds, blanched and finely chopped
½  cup shallots or green onion, chopped
¼  cup tomato, chopped
8   sole fillets, fresh or frozen
2   tablespoons lemon juice
    Milk-free bread crumbs
    Milk-free margarine

Melt margarine in a frying pan and sauté the onion, almonds, shallots, and tomato for 1 minute. Set aside. Rinse the fillets in cold water. Roll loosely and stand each fillet upright in a cup of a muffin tin. Fill the fillets with the nut mixture, pour on a little lemon juice, sprinkle with bread crumbs, and dot with margarine. Bake fillets in the muffin tin at 375° for about 30 minutes.

| Each serving provides: | | | |
|---|---|---|---|
| 494 | Calories | 16 g | Carbohydrate |
| 36 g | Protein | 526 mg | Sodium |
| 32 g | Fat | 82 mg | Cholesterol |

# Baked Fillet of Flounder

*Makes 1 Serving*

1    flounder fillet
1    tablespoon lemon juice
½    teaspoon mayonnaise
1    tablespoon milk-free bread crumbs
     Milk-free margarine
     Salt (optional)

Rinse the fillet and lay flat in a greased baking dish. Pour lemon juice over fish. Spread mayonnaise on top, and sprinkle with bread crumbs. Dot with margarine. Sprinkle with salt if desired. Bake uncovered at 350° for 40 minutes or until bread crumbs are toasty. Adjust for multiple servings.

| Each serving provides: | | | |
|---|---|---|---|
| 216 | Calories | 6 g | Carbohydrate |
| 33 g | Protein | 222 mg | Sodium |
| 6 g | Fat | 83 mg | Cholesterol |

# Mandarin Shrimp

*Makes 12 Servings (2½ per serving)*

| | |
|---|---|
| 2 | tablespoons olive oil |
| 1 | teaspoon garlic, minced |
| 30 | peeled and deveined medium-sized shrimp |
| ½ | pound cashews |
| 1 | green onion, chopped |
| 2 | tablespoons soy sauce |
| 1 | tablespoon cornstarch |
| 1 | 6-ounce can of mandarin oranges, drained (reserve juice) |
| | Salt and pepper to taste |

Heat oil until hot. Add garlic and stir until lightly browned. Add shrimp and cook until just pink. Add cashews, onion, soy sauce. In a separate bowl blend cornstarch with 1 cup reserved mandarin orange juice. Bring shrimp mixture to a boil and thicken with cornstarch/juice mixture. Reduce to simmer. Add salt and pepper. Add oranges. Serve at once.

---

Each serving provides:

| | | | |
|---|---|---|---|
| 202 | Calories | 3 g | Carbohydrate |
| 15 g | Protein | 260 mg | Sodium |
| 12 g | Fat | 87 mg | Cholesterol |

# Shrimp Pâté

*Makes 8 Servings*

| | |
|---|---|
| 1 | pound cooked shrimp |
| ⅓ | cup milk-free margarine |
| ½ | cup mayonnaise |
| 3 | tablespoons green onion, chopped |
| 2 | teaspoons sherry |
| 1½ | teaspoons Dijon mustard |
| ¼ | teaspoon pepper |

In a food processor or blender, combine shrimp and margarine until it forms a stiff paste. Add the remaining ingredients and blend well. Chill thoroughly.

---

Each serving provides:

| 177 | Calories | .50 g | Carbohydrate |
|---|---|---|---|
| 12 g | Protein | 283 mg | Sodium |
| 14 g | Fat | 115 mg | Cholesterol |

# Shrimp de Jonghe

*Makes 12 Servings*

½   cup milk-free margarine
1   clove garlic, chopped fine
¼   cup parsley flakes (or chopped, fresh)
½   teaspoon paprika
¼   teaspoon white pepper
½   cup dry white wine
1½  cups milk-free bread crumbs
4   cups cooked shrimp

In a small saucepan, on very low heat, melt margarine and add garlic, parsley, paprika, and pepper. Slowly stir in wine and blend well. Pour bread crumbs into a medium-sized bowl; add margarine mixture and mix well. Spread shrimp in a 9-inch square baking dish. Cover with bread crumb mixture. Bake at 350° for 25 minutes, or until well browned.

---

Each serving provides:

| 175 | Calories | 10 g | Carbohydrate |
|-----|----------|------|--------------|
| 14 g | Protein | 310 mg | Sodium |
| 9 g | Fat | 112 mg | Cholesterol |

# Shrimp in Pita

*Makes 4 Servings*

1     avocado, mashed
2     teaspoons chives, chopped
1     teaspoon lime or lemon juice
½     cup cucumber, chopped
1     tablespoon mayonnaise
      Salt and pepper to taste
1     cup cooked shrimp, diced
2     small rounds of pita bread

In a small bowl, mix avocado, chives, lime juice, and cucumber. Add mayonnaise and blend well. Add salt and pepper. Gently blend in shrimp. Heat pita bread in an oven set at 350° for 10 minutes. Cut each pita round in half and stuff pockets with shrimp mixture.

| Each serving provides: | | | |
|---|---|---|---|
| 251 | Calories | 23 g | Carbohydrate |
| 16 g | Protein | 334 mg | Sodium |
| 11 g | Fat | 113 mg | Cholesterol |

# Seafood en Brochette

*Makes 6 Servings*

6   large shelled and deveined shrimp
1   pound large scallops
1   large green pepper, seeded and cut into 2-inch pieces
½   pound fresh pineapple, cut into small wedges
12  cherry tomatoes
1   medium onion, cut into 6 wedges

Marinade:

½   cup sherry
2   tablespoons sesame seed oil
1   tablespoon sesame seeds
1   clove garlic, finely chopped

Combine all the ingredients for the marinade in a bowl. Add the shrimp and scallops, marinating at room temperature for 30 minutes. Drain, reserving the remaining marinade. On 6 skewers, alternate the seafood with the fruit and vegetables. Broil or grill the brochettes about 4 inches from the heat for 8-10 minutes. Turn and brush often with the rest of the marinade.

| Each serving provides: | | | |
|---|---|---|---|
| 151 | Calories | 11 g | Carbohydrate |
| 18 g | Protein | 160 mg | Sodium |
| 4 g | Fat | 60 mg | Cholesterol |

# Creamed Fettuccine with Crab

*Makes 8 Servings (2 ounces per serving)*

8    ounces spinach fettuccine
8    ounces white fettuccine
2    cups milk-free White Sauce #1 (page 141)
½    pound crab meat, flaked
     Salt and pepper to taste

Cook pasta according to directions. Prepare white sauce. Shred crab meat and add to sauce. Drain fettuccine and pour into a serving bowl. Toss with crab sauce, adding salt and pepper as desired.

---

Each serving provides:

| 298 | Calories | 43 g | Carbohydrate |
|---|---|---|---|
| 15 g | Protein | 368 mg | Sodium |
| 8 g | Fat | 116 mg | Cholesterol |

# Oven-Fried Scallops

*Makes 2 Servings*

½   pound large scallops
¾   cup milk-free bread crumbs
½   teaspoon salt
¼   teaspoon white pepper
¼   teaspoon paprika
2   eggs (or substitute), beaten

Rinse scallops in cold water. Mix together bread crumbs, salt, pepper, and paprika. Dip each scallop in egg and then roll in bread-crumb mixture. Place scallops on an oiled cookie sheet and bake at 450° for about 12 minutes. Scallops should be crisp on the outside and soft on the inside. Adjust recipe for multiple servings.

| Each serving provides: | | | |
|---|---|---|---|
| 328 | Calories | 31 g | Carbohydrate |
| 30 g | Protein | 1075 mg | Sodium |
| 8 g | Fat | 314 mg | Cholesterol |

# Eggs and Pancakes

## Fiesta Eggs

*Makes 10 Servings*

| | |
|---|---|
| 12 | eggs |
| ½ | cup water |
| 4 | tablespoons milk-free margarine |
| 1 | teaspoon black pepper |
| 10 | prepared soft tortillas |
| 1 | 12-ounce jar picante sauce (mild or hot) |

In a large bowl, beat eggs with water until light yellow and very foamy. Melt margarine in a large frying pan. On very low heat, gently cook eggs, tossing with a wooden spoon. Add pepper and blend well. In the center of each tortilla, place a scoop of about ¾ cup egg mixture. Roll up the sides and align in a 9 × 13-inch baking pan. Spoon about half the picante sauce over the tops of the filled tortillas and heat in a 350° oven about 20 minutes. Serve with additional sauce.

| Each serving provides: | | | |
|---|---|---|---|
| 262 | Calories | 27 g | Carbohydrate |
| 11 g | Protein | 575 mg | Sodium |
| 12 g | Fat | 329 mg | Cholesterol |

# Eggs Benedict

*Makes 4 Servings*

4   slices grilled ham
4   slices milk-free toast
4   eggs, poached
    Hollandaise Sauce

Place a slice of ham over each piece of toast. Top with a poached egg and pour on Hollandaise Sauce.

Note: To poach an egg, bring 3 inches of water to a boil in a small saucepan, then turn the heat to low. Stir the water to create a well in the center and slip the egg into the well. Cook the egg for 3-5 minutes, depending on your preference for doneness. Remove the egg with a slotted spoon.

| Each serving provides: | | | |
|---|---|---|---|
| 357 | Calories | 20 g | Carbohydrate |
| 17 g | Protein | 912 mg | Sodium |
| 23 g | Fat | 392 mg | Cholesterol |

# Company Scrambled Eggs

*Makes 6 Servings*

| | |
|---|---|
| 12 | eggs |
| ½ | cup water |
| ¼ | cup milk substitute |
| ½ | teaspoon salt |
| ¼ | teaspoon pepper |
| ¼ | teaspoon dill |
| ¼ | teaspoon oregano |
| 3 | tablespoons milk-free margarine |

Beat eggs with a wire whisk. Add all other ingredients except margarine and beat again until very frothy. Melt margarine in a large frying pan and cook eggs over low heat, turning occasionally. Remove when fully cooked, yet still moist.

Note: Excellent when served with sautéed chicken livers, sautéed onions, or sautéed green pepper slices.

| Each serving provides: | | | |
|---|---|---|---|
| 223 | Calories | 2 g | Carbohydrate |
| 12 g | Protein | 395 mg | Sodium |
| 18 g | Fat | 548 mg | Cholesterol |

# Deviled Eggs

*Makes 4 Servings*

6    eggs, hard-boiled
2    tablespoons pickle relish
1    tablespoon mayonnaise
1    tablespoon Dijon mustard
½    teaspoon Worcestershire sauce
¼    teaspoon salt
     Paprika

Cut eggs in half lengthwise and remove yolks. Add remaining ingredients to yolks and blend until smooth. Refill egg whites and sprinkle with paprika.

| Each serving provides: | | | |
|---|---|---|---|
| 159 | Calories | 4 g | Carbohydrate |
| 9 g | Protein | 432 mg | Sodium |
| 11 g | Fat | 413 mg | Cholesterol |

# Spanish Omelet

*Makes 2 Servings*

| | |
|---|---|
| 6 | eggs, separated |
| ⅓ | cup water |
| ½ | teaspoon salt |
| 3 | tablespoons milk-free margarine |
| ¼ | cup green pepper, chopped |
| ¼ | cup tomato, chopped |
| 1 | tablespoon onion, minced |

Beat the egg whites until bubbly. Add water and salt and beat until thick. In a separate bowl, beat the yolks until very thick and lemon colored. Fold yolks into whites. Melt half the margarine in a frying pan. When a drop of water sizzles in the pan, pour in half of the egg mixture. Reduce heat and cook until bottom is browned. Add half of the vegetables, and fold omelet over. Finish cooking on both sides. Remove omelet from pan and repeat the process with the remaining ingredients.

| Each serving provides: | | | |
|---|---|---|---|
| 399 | Calories | 4 g | Carbohydrate |
| 19 g | Protein | 957 mg | Sodium |
| 34 g | Fat | 822 mg | Cholesterol |

# French Toast

*Makes 3 Servings*

2    eggs
¼    cup milk substitute
¼    cup water
6    slices milk-free bread
     Milk-free margarine

Beat eggs in a shallow bowl. Add milk substitute and water. Beat until frothy. Soak each slice of bread in egg mixture, first on one side, then the other. Cook both sides in a well-greased frying pan until golden.

Note: For an interesting twist, substitute orange or pineapple juice for water/milk substitute combination.

|  | Each serving provides: | | |
|---|---|---|---|
| 351 | Calories | 42 g | Carbohydrate |
| 11 g | Protein | 557 mg | Sodium |
| 15 g | Fat | 185 mg | Cholesterol |

# Presidential French Toast

*Makes 4 Servings*

| | |
|---|---|
| 6 | eggs |
| ⅔ | cup orange juice |
| ⅓ | cup Grand Marnier |
| ⅓ | cup milk substitute |
| 3 | tablespoons sugar |
| ¼ | teaspoon vanilla |
| ¼ | teaspoon salt |
| 8 | ¾-inch slices white bread |

Beat together the eggs, juice, liqueur, milk substitute, sugar, vanilla, and salt. Dip bread into mixture, coating all sides. Transfer to a baking dish in a single layer. Pour any remaining liquid on top. Cover and refrigerate overnight. To cook, melt milk-free margarine in a large frying pan. Brown well on both sides. Cut diagonally and serve.

| Each serving provides: | | | |
|---|---|---|---|
| 377 | Calories | 52 g | Carbohydrate |
| 14 g | Protein | 559 mg | Sodium |
| 12 g | Fat | 413 mg | Cholesterol |

# Pancakes

*Makes 4 Servings*

1     cup flour
1     tablespoon baking powder
1     tablespoon sugar
½     teaspoon salt
1     beaten egg (or substitute)
½     cup orange juice
½     cup water
2     tablespoons vegetable oil
      Milk-free margarine for griddle

Mix together dry ingredients. Combine egg, orange juice, water, and oil. Add liquid to dry ingredients, stirring just until moist. Let mixture rest for 30 seconds. Spoon or pour batter onto greased, hot griddle. Cook pancakes on the first side until bubbles appear on upper surface. Turn over and cook until bottom is golden.

| Each serving provides: | | | |
|---|---|---|---|
| 273 | Calories | 31 g | Carbohydrate |
| 5 g | Protein | 678 mg | Sodium |
| 14 g | Fat | 69 mg | Cholesterol |

# Crêpes

*Makes 18 Servings*

3      eggs
1      teaspoon salt
½      cup water
1½     cups flour
1      cup water
       Milk-free margarine, melted

Beat eggs, salt, and ½ cup water with a wire whisk. Add flour and 1 cup water, and beat until thoroughly blended. Heat a 4- or 5-inch skillet on low flame and brush with enough melted milk-free margarine to grease the bottom of the pan. Pour in about 2 tablespoons batter and turn the pan so that the batter spreads over the entire bottom. Pour off excess batter. Cook on one side until the top is dry. Turn onto a paper towel. Continue this process until all the batter is gone. Crêpes may be frozen.

Note: For dessert crêpes, gently turn and cook on the other side before removing from the skillet.

| | Each serving provides: | | |
|---|---|---|---|
| 68 | Calories | 8 g | Carbohydrate |
| 2 g | Protein | 156 mg | Sodium |
| 3 g | Fat | 46 mg | Cholesterol |

# Flaming Crêpes

*Makes 18 Servings*

Prepare one recipe of crêpes, turning to brown both sides. Set aside.

# Fresh Fruit Filling

½   cup water

½   cup sugar

2    cups fresh peaches or nectarines, cut into chunks

1    pint fresh blueberries

2    cups fresh pears

½   cup Triplesec Liqueur

In a large saucepan, combine water and sugar. Stir over low heat until blended. Add fruit and cook until softened. Add liqueur. Light a match to this mixture to flame. When finished, fill crêpes and serve. Top with juices from the fruit mixture.

| Each serving provides: | | | |
|---|---|---|---|
| 126 | Calories | 23 g | Carbohydrate |
| 3 g | Protein | 158 mg | Sodium |
| 3 g | Fat | 46 mg | Cholesterol |

# Fruits and Vegetables

## Fruit Soufflé

*Makes 12 Servings*

1   16-ounce can unsweetened pears

1   16-ounce can unsweetened peaches

1   13.25-ounce can unsweetened pineapple chunks

1   15-ounce can mandarin oranges (reserve juice)

⅓   cup milk-free margarine

¾   cup light brown sugar

1   tablespoon cornstarch

¼   cup fruit juice (mandarin orange)

¼   cup Cointreau

Drain cans of fruit, reserving juice from oranges. Put fruit in a 10 × 15-inch baking dish and combine well. In a small pot, melt the margarine and add brown sugar. Combine cornstarch and mandarin orange juice and add to margarine/sugar mixture. Simmer until sugar melts and a thick sauce is formed. Add Cointreau and blend. Pour this sauce over fruit and bake at 325° for about 40 minutes.

| Each serving provides: | | | |
|---|---|---|---|
| 180 | Calories | 35 g | Carbohydrate |
| .68 g | Protein | 68 mg | Sodium |
| 5 g | Fat | 00 mg | Cholesterol |

# Strawberry Yogurt

*Makes 4 Servings*

1       10.5-ounce cake soft tofu
1½      teaspoons vanilla
1½      tablespoons lemon juice
1       10-ounce package frozen strawberries

Purée tofu in blender. Add the vanilla, lemon juice, and strawberries. Sweeten, if desired. Serve chilled. Only keeps in the refrigerator a short time (6-8 hours).

| Each serving provides: | | | |
|---|---|---|---|
| 88 | Calories | 9 g | Carbohydrate |
| 6 g | Protein | 8 mg | Sodium |
| 4 g | Fat | 00 mg | Cholesterol |

# Vegetable Pâté

*Makes 4 Servings*

2   medium onions, chopped
2   tablespoons milk-free margarine
1   16-ounce can green beans, drained
2   hard-boiled eggs
⅓   cup cashews

On low heat, sauté onions in margarine until transparent. Blend all ingredients together, including onions, in a food processor or blender until well-puréed. Season to taste, using salt, pepper, and garlic powder. Chill thoroughly.

---

Each serving provides:

| 183 | Calories | | 10 g | Carbohydrate |
|---|---|---|---|---|
| 6 g | Protein | | 281 mg | Sodium |
| 14 g | Fat | | 137 mg | Cholesterol |

# Squash Relish

*Makes 8 Servings*

| | |
|---|---|
| 1 | pound yellow squash, unpeeled, sliced |
| 1 | pound zucchini, unpeeled, sliced |
| 1 | lemon, sliced thin and cut in halves |
| 1 | red pepper, sliced |
| ½ | cup sliced Bermuda onion |
| 2 | teaspoons salt |
| 2 | teaspoons celery seed |
| ¾ | cup sugar |
| ½ | cup lemon juice |

Toss the first 7 ingredients. Let stand 1 hour. In a small bowl combine sugar and lemon juice. Stir until sugar is dissolved. Pour over vegetables and refrigerate, covered, at least 24 hours before serving.

---

Each serving provides:

| 105 | Calories | 26 g | Carbohydrate |
|---|---|---|---|
| 2 g | Protein | 558 mg | Sodium |
| .47 g | Fat | 00 mg | Cholesterol |

# Ratatouille

*Makes 8 Servings*

| | |
|---|---|
| 3 | tablespoons olive oil |
| 3 | small onions, peeled and chopped |
| 1 | small green pepper, seeded and cut into strips |
| ½ | small eggplant, peeled, sliced, and cut into strips |
| 1 | small zucchini, peeled and cut into strips |
| 2 | small tomatoes, cut into wedges |
| 1 | pound fresh mushrooms |
| | Salt and pepper |

Heat oil in skillet and sauté onions and green pepper until lightly browned. Add more oil and sauté eggplant. Remove and reserve. Do the same to the other vegetables, adding a bit more oil as necessary. Combine all ingredients in a baking dish and bake at 400° for 30 minutes, uncovered. If dish appears to be getting dry, cover with foil. May be served either hot or cold.

Each serving provides:

| 78 | Calories | 7 g | Carbohydrate |
|---|---|---|---|
| 2 g | Protein | 6 mg | Sodium |
| 5 g | Fat | 00 mg | Cholesterol |

# Squash and Pear Bake

*Makes 6 Servings*

1    large butternut squash
1    16-ounce can pear halves in light syrup
½    cup brown sugar
2    tablespoons milk-free margarine

Bake whole squash at 375° for about 45 minutes, until tender but still somewhat firm. If using a microwave, slash squash with a knife before cooking. Remove skin and slice into ½-inch slices, discarding seeds. Grease a glass baking dish. Place in the dish alternately, 1 piece of squash and 1 pear half until the dish is full. Sprinkle with brown sugar and dot with margarine. Bake at 325° for 30 minutes, or until squash is completely soft and topping is slightly browned.

---

Each serving provides:

| 214 | Calories | 44 g | Carbohydrate |
|---|---|---|---|
| 1 g | Protein | 72 mg | Sodium |
| 5 g | Fat | 3 mg | Cholesterol |

# Remarkable Beans

*Makes 8 Servings*

| | |
|---|---|
| 2 | cans northern beans with liquid |
| ¼ | cup chopped parsley (fresh is preferred) |
| ½ | cup grated onion |
| ¼ | cup tarragon vinegar |
| ½ | teaspoon salt |
| ¼ | teaspoon pepper |
| ½ | teaspoon garlic powder |

Combine all the ingredients and marinate in the refrigerator at least 48 hours. Serve very cold.

---

Each serving provides:

| 128 | Calories | 24 g | Carbohydrate |
|---|---|---|---|
| 8 g | Protein | 142 mg | Sodium |
| .45 g | Fat | 00 mg | Cholesterol |

# Green Bean Casserole

*Makes 8 Servings*

½   pound green beans, cut into 1-inch pieces
½   cup mushrooms, sliced
1    cube Telma mushroom soup (Kosher and pareve)
¾   cup cold water
¼   cup milk substitute
¾   cup cornflake crumbs or crushed croutons

Toss beans and mushrooms in a 1-quart casserole. In a small saucepan, crush cube of mushroom soup in the water, and add milk substitute. Bring to a boil and simmer for 5 minutes. Pour soup over beans and mushrooms, and top with crumbs. Bake at 350° for 1 hour. Add some water if casserole becomes dry.

|  | Each serving provides: |  |  |
|---|---|---|---|
| 64 | Calories | 13 g | Carbohydrate |
| 2 g | Protein | 568 mg | Sodium |
| 1 g | Fat | 00 mg | Cholesterol |

# Scalloped Potatoes

*Makes 6 Servings*

3    tablespoons milk-free margarine

2    tablespoons flour

6    potatoes, sliced, washed, and drained

½    cup green onion, chopped

¼    teaspoon salt

½    cup milk substitute

1    cup water

     Paprika

     Milk-free bread crumbs

Grease a 1-quart casserole dish. Arrange a layer of potatoes on the bottom. Mix together the flour and salt. Sprinkle over the potatoes and dot with margarine. Sprinkle some chopped onion on top. Add a layer of potatoes and continue this procedure until the casserole is full. Mix milk substitute with water and pour over. Top with paprika and bread crumbs. Bake at 400° for 1 hour.

| Each serving provides: | | | |
|---|---|---|---|
| 207 | Calories | 31 g | Carbohydrate |
| 4 g | Protein | 211 mg | Sodium |
| 8 g | Fat | .20 mg | Cholesterol |

# Double-Baked Potatoes

*Makes 4 Servings*

4       medium baking potatoes
¼       cup milk-free margarine
½       cup milk substitute
        Salt and pepper
        Garlic powder

Wash potatoes, and prick with a fork. Bake at 375° for 45 minutes, or until soft. Slice off about ½ inch across the top of each potato and discard tops. Scoop contents of each potato into a large mixing bowl. Add margarine, milk substitute, salt, pepper, and garlic powder to taste. Beat with an electric mixer at high speed for 2 minutes. Mix with any of the suggested Mixers and refill the potato skins, or refill the skins with just the beaten potatoes. Top with any of the suggested Toppers. Rebake potatoes at 425° until crusty, about 10-15 minutes.

## Mixers

Prepared mustard
Dijon mustard
Dill
Sweet pickle relish
Chili sauce

## Toppers

Cornflake crumbs
Crumbled Italian sausage
Bacon bits
Crushed croutons

| Each serving provides: | | | |
|---|---|---|---|
| 268 | Calories | 32 g | Carbohydrate |
| 4 g | Protein | 169 mg | Sodium |
| 15 g | Fat | 00 mg | Cholesterol |

# Potato Pancakes

*Makes 6 Servings*

6-8   medium potatoes

1     tablespoon onion, minced

2     eggs

3     tablespoons flour

1     teaspoon salt

½     teaspoon baking powder

Peel and grate potatoes. Add onion and let mixture stand about 15 minutes. Pour off liquid.* Beat eggs slightly and blend into potato mixture. Add dry ingredients and mix well. Cook spoonfuls of mixture in a hot, well-oiled skillet. Serve with cold applesauce, Hot Apple-Pear Sauce, or cinnamon and sugar.

*May be made in a blender.

| Each serving provides: | | | |
|---|---|---|---|
| 219 | Calories | 30 g | Carbohydrate |
| 6 g | Protein | 434 mg | Sodium |
| 9 g | Fat | 91 mg | Cholesterol |

# Potato Soufflé

*Makes 12 Servings*

| | |
|---|---|
| 3 | pounds potatoes |
| ½ | cup milk substitute |
| ¼ | cup water |
| 1 | teaspoon salt |
| ¼ | teaspoon white pepper |
| 2 | egg yolks, beaten |
| 4 | tablespoons milk-free margarine |
| 2 | egg whites, stiffly beaten |

Cook potatoes in jackets until soft. Drain and peel. Mash thoroughly. Heat milk substitute and water and set aside until tepid. Blend seasonings, egg yolks, and 3 tablespoons margarine until potatoes are well seasoned. Add enough milk substitute and water mixture to make potatoes creamy. Beat well, using a hand mixer if desired. Fold in egg whites and pour mixture into a well-greased 2-quart casserole. Dot with remaining margarine. Bake at 375° for 30 minutes, or until browned.

| Each serving provides: | | | |
|---|---|---|---|
| 192 | Calories | 25 g | Carbohydrate |
| 4 g | Protein | 376 mg | Sodium |
| 9 g | Fat | 68 mg | Cholesterol |

# Broccolied Potatoes

*Makes 8 Servings*

12   small red potatoes, cooked and cut into quarters
1    9-ounce package frozen cut broccoli, thawed and well
     drained
½    cup vegetable oil
¼    cup cider vinegar
2    tablespoons lemon juice
1    teaspoon onion powder
1    teaspoon sugar
½    teaspoon freshly snipped parsley

Combine all ingredients and cover. Refrigerate at least 2 hours. Serve cold.

---

Each serving provides:

| 191 | Calories | 18 g | Carbohydrate |
|-----|----------|------|--------------|
| 3 g | Protein | 15 mg | Sodium |
| 14 g | Fat | 00 mg | Cholesterol |

# Bronze Carrots

*Makes 8 Servings*

| | |
|---|---|
| 2 | pounds fresh carrots |
| 1 | 10-ounce can tomato soup |
| 1 | cup sugar |
| ½ | cup olive oil |
| ½ | cup vinegar |
| 1 | tablespoon prepared mustard |
| 1 | tablespoon Worcestershire sauce |
| 1 | green pepper, cut into thin strips |
| 1 | medium onion, sliced thin |

Clean and cut carrots into 1-inch slices. Steam until soft. In a saucepan combine the remaining ingredients. Bring to a boil and cook on medium heat about 2 minutes. Chill, stirring occasionally. Add carrots to sauce and refrigerate in a tightly covered container. Serve in 24 hours. Will keep 3-4 weeks in refrigerator. Serve cold.

| Each serving provides: | | | |
|---|---|---|---|
| 294 | Calories | 42 g | Carbohydrate |
| 2 g | Protein | 328 mg | Sodium |
| 14 g | Fat | 00 mg | Cholesterol |

# Veggie Cutlets

*Makes 4 Servings*

1    cup minced onion

1    cup minced celery

1    package frozen mixed vegetables, thawed and drained

½    cup mayonnaise

1    egg or egg white, beaten
     Milk-free margarine

Mix all ingredients together. Cover and chill at least 2 hours. Shape into 4 patties. In a skillet, heat 2 tablespoons milk-free margarine. Cook patties, turning once, until well browned.

| Each serving provides: | | | |
|---|---|---|---|
| 337 | Calories | 14 g | Carbohydrate |
| 5 g | Protein | 301 mg | Sodium |
| 29 g | Fat | 85 mg | Cholesterol |

# Hungarian Cabbage Strudel

*Makes 12 Servings*

8   slices bacon, chopped
5   cups chopped cabbage
1   cup chopped onion
1   tablespoon horseradish
    Salt and pepper to taste
1   package phyllo dough
6   tablespoons melted milk-free margarine

In a large skillet, sauté bacon until crisp. Drain off fat, leaving about 2 tablespoons in the pan. Add cabbage, onions, horseradish, and seasonings. Cover. Cook on low heat until soft, stirring occasionally, about 20 minutes. Use 6 sheets of phyllo dough, two sheets for each strudel. Brush melted margarine on each. Spread ⅓ of the filling on two sheets of dough lengthwise and roll like a jelly roll. Tuck the seam under and place on a large cookie sheet. Repeat with remaining dough and filling. With a sharp knife, score the top lightly into serving-sized slices, being careful not to cut through more than two or three layers. Brush with melted margarine. Bake at 375° for 25 minutes or until golden brown.

|  | Each serving provides: |  |  |
|---|---|---|---|
| 207 | Calories | 28 g | Carbohydrate |
| 6 g | Protein | 141 mg | Sodium |
| 8 g | Fat | 4 mg | Cholesterol |

# Spinach Quiche

*Makes 8 Servings*

| | |
|---|---|
| 1 | 10-ounce package frozen chopped spinach |
| 4 | tablespoons flour |
| 4 | tablespoons milk-free margarine |
| 1½ | cups milk substitute |
| 3 | eggs, well beaten |
| 1 | carrot, grated |
| 1 | onion, chopped |
| ½ | teaspoon garlic powder |
| 1 | teaspoon dill |
| 1 | 9-inch unbaked pie shell |

Thaw spinach. Melt margarine over low heat. Add flour and stir until smooth. Add milk substitute and continue stirring. Slowly add eggs; then add spinach, other vegetables, and spices. Mix well and pour into pie shell. Bake at 375° for 40 minutes.

---

Each serving provides:

| 364 | Calories | 28 g | Carbohydrate |
|---|---|---|---|
| 7g | Protein | 295 mg | Sodium |
| 25 g | Fat | 103 mg | Cholesterol |

# Vegetables Julienne

*Makes 4 Servings*

2    small zucchini, sliced into thin strips
6    carrots, peeled and sliced into thin strips
½    cup chopped green onion
2    tablespoons milk-free margarine
3    tablespoons soy sauce
1    tablespoon brown sugar

Prepare vegetables and set aside. In a saucepan, melt margarine and mix well with soy sauce. On high heat, stir-fry zucchini. Remove and set aside. Do the same with the carrots. Replace the zucchini and sprinkle with onion. Stir-fry for about 30 seconds to blend flavors. Sprinkle brown sugar on top and cook another 30 seconds. Serve immediately.

|  | Each serving provides: | | |
|---|---|---|---|
| 128 | Calories | 18 g | Carbohydrate |
| 3 g | Protein | 879 mg | Sodium |
| 6 g | Fat | 00 mg | Cholesterol |

# Vegetable Soufflé

*Makes 4 Servings*

3  eggs, separated
½  cup White Sauce #2 (page 142)
1  cup frozen mixed vegetables, cooked and chopped
  Salt and pepper to taste

Beat egg yolks until thick. Add white sauce and blend well. Add vegetables and seasoning. Beat egg whites until stiff. Gently fold in vegetable mixture. Pour into a greased 2-cup baking or soufflé dish. Bake at 325° for about 40-50 minutes.

| Each serving provides: | | | |
|---|---|---|---|
| 155 | Calories | 11 g | Carbohydrate |
| 7 g | Protein | 192 mg | Sodium |
| 10 g | Fat | 206 mg | Cholesterol |

# Easiest Marinated Vegetables

Fill plastic bags with different vegetables, one type to a bag. Pour in enough of your favorite Italian dressing or vinaigrette to cover vegetables. Tie bags and refrigerate overnight. Before serving, poke a hole in the bottom of each bag and let the marinade drain out. Discard bags. Arrange vegetables on a tray and serve cold. Try the following:

Green beans, raw or canned
Sliced zucchini (raw)
Hearts of palm (canned)
Cherry tomatoes (raw)
Cooked carrots
Kidney beans (cooked)
Lima beans (cooked)
Fresh mushrooms (whole)
Fresh cauliflowerets
Fresh broccoli spears (or cooked)
Sliced jicama

# Couscous

*Makes 6 Servings*

| | |
|---|---|
| 1 | small onion |
| ½ | cup chopped green pepper |
| ½ | cup chopped celery |
| 2 | tablespoons milk-free margarine |
| 1 | 9½-ounce box of toasted couscous |
| ½ | cup water |
| | Salt and pepper to taste |
| 2 | cubes chicken bouillon |

Sauté onion, green pepper, and celery in margarine. In a saucepan, cover and simmer couscous with water, salt and pepper, and bouillon until all the water is absorbed. Add sautéed vegetables and toss. Serve hot or cold.

---

Each serving provides:

| 195 | Calories | 35 g | Carbohydrate |
|---|---|---|---|
| 6 g | Protein | 429 mg | Sodium |
| 4 g | Fat | .19 mg | Cholesterol |

# Cakes and Frostings

## Chocolate Cake

*Makes 16 Servings*

| | |
|---|---|
| ⅔ | cup milk-free margarine |
| 1⅔ | cups sugar |
| 3 | eggs |
| ½ | teaspoon vanilla |
| 2 | cups flour |
| ⅔ | cup cocoa powder |
| 1¼ | teaspoon baking soda |
| 1 | teaspoon salt |
| ¼ | teaspoon baking powder |
| 1⅓ | cups water |

Place first 4 ingredients in mixing bowl and beat on high for 3 minutes. Combine dry ingredients and add alternately with water to creamed mixture. Pour into 2 greased and cocoa-powdered 9-inch round baking pans. Bake at 350° for 30-35 minutes. Let cakes cool in pans for 10 minutes. Invert onto wire racks to cool completely. Frost or glaze, or dust with confectioners' sugar.

| Each serving provides: | | | |
|---|---|---|---|
| 230 | Calories | 35 g | Carbohydrate |
| 3 g | Protein | 311 mg | Sodium |
| 10 g | Fat | 51 mg | Cholesterol |

# Chocolate Mousse Cake

*Makes 16 Servings*

2   packages prepared milk-free ladyfingers
1   recipe Chocolate Mousse (page 278)
1   6-ounce package semi-sweet chocolate bits (optional)

Line a springform pan with upright ladyfingers. Pour the mousse into the pan and refrigerate for several hours or overnight. Release the cake and top with semi-sweet chocolate bits, if desired.

---

Each serving provides:

| 197 | Calories | | 28 g | Carbohydrate |
|-----|----------|---|------|--------------|
| 3 g | Protein | | 96 mg | Sodium |
| 9 g | Fat | | 123 mg | Cholesterol |

# Chocolate Chip-Applesauce Cake

*Makes 8 Servings*

| | |
|---|---|
| 1¾ | cups flour |
| 1 | teaspoon baking soda |
| ¼ | teaspoon salt |
| 1 | teaspoon cinnamon |
| ½ | cup shortening |
| 1 | cup sugar |
| 2 | eggs |
| 1 | cup applesauce |
| ½ | cup raisins |
| ½ | cup chopped nuts |
| 1 | cup chocolate chips |

Sift together flour, baking soda, salt, and cinnamon. In a separate bowl, cream shortening and sugar. Add eggs, one at a time, beating well after each one. Alternately, add flour mixture and applesauce to creamed mixture, beating well after each addition until smooth. Stir in raisins, nuts, and half of the chocolate chips. Pour batter into a greased 9-inch loaf pan. Sprinkle remainder of chocolate chips over batter. Bake at 325° for 1-1½ hours, or until well browned. Let cool in pan. Cover tightly with plastic wrap and store overnight before cutting.

---

Each serving provides:

| | | | |
|---|---|---|---|
| 537 | Calories | 73 g | Carbohydrate |
| 7 g | Protein | 192 mg | Sodium |
| 26 g | Fat | 69 mg | Cholesterol |

# Pineapple-Upside-Down Cake

*Makes 12 Servings*

3       tablespoons milk-free margarine

¾       cup brown sugar

1       8½-ounce can sliced pineapple in light syrup, drained
        (reserve syrup)

⅓       cup milk-free margarine, softened

½       cup sugar

1       egg

1½      teaspoons vanilla

1       cup flour

1½      teaspoons baking powder

¼       teaspoon salt

In a small pan, melt 3 tablespoons margarine. Add brown sugar and 1 tablespoon pineapple syrup. Set aside. Cream together ⅓ cup margarine and white sugar. Add egg and vanilla and beat until fluffy. Sift together flour, baking powder, and salt, and add to creamed mixture alternately with remaining pineapple syrup. Using either an 8-inch square or 9-inch round baking pan, pour in brown sugar and margarine mixture. Arrange pineapple slices in the ungreased pan and cover with batter. Bake at 350° for about 40 minutes. Cool 5 minutes and invert onto a serving plate.

| Each serving provides: | | | |
|---|---|---|---|
| 211 | Calories | 33 g | Carbohydrate |
| 2 g | Protein | 192 mg | Sodium |
| 9 g | Fat | 23 mg | Cholesterol |

# Sponge Cake
### *Makes 12 Servings*

| | |
|---|---|
| 1½ | cups sifted flour |
| 1½ | cups sugar |
| ¼ | teaspoon salt |
| ½ | teaspoon baking powder |
| 6 | eggs, separated |
| 1 | teaspoon cream of tartar |
| ¼ | cup cold water |
| 1 | teaspoon vanilla |
| 2 | teaspoons lemon juice |
| 2 | teaspoons lemon rind, grated |

In a small bowl, sift together flour, 1 cup sugar, salt, and baking powder. In a large bowl, combine egg whites and cream of tartar. Beat until thick. Slowly add ½ cup sugar and beat until mixture is stiff. In a small bowl, combine egg yolks, water, vanilla, lemon juice, and grated rind. Add this to dry mixture and beat about 1 minute. Fold slowly into egg whites, blending well. Pour into an ungreased 10-inch tube pan. Bake at 350° for 40-45 minutes. Invert pan and cool for 1 hour before removing cake from pan.

---

Each serving provides:

| | | | |
|---|---|---|---|
| 190 | Calories | 36 g | Carbohydrate |
| 5 g | Protein | 98 mg | Sodium |
| 3 g | Fat | 137 mg | Cholesterol |

# Orange Chiffon Cake

*Makes 12 Servings*

| 6 | egg whites |
|---|---|
| 1½ | cups sugar |
| 6 | egg yolks |
| 1¾ | cups sifted flour |
| ½ | teaspoon salt |
| 6 | tablespoons fresh orange juice |
| 1 | tablespoon grated orange peel |
| | Confectioners' sugar |

Beat egg whites until foamy. Gradually beat in ½ cup sugar and continue beating until stiff peaks form. Set aside. In a small bowl, beat egg yolks at high speed until very thick and lemon colored, at least 3 minutes. Gradually beat in remaining 1 cup sugar. Beat until smooth. Combine flour and salt. Add alternately to egg mixture with orange juice. Begin and end with flour mixture. With a spatula, blend in orange peel. Fold yolk mixture into whites. Pour batter into an ungreased 10-inch tube pan. Bake at 350° about 35 minutes. Cake is done when it springs back to the touch. Cool completely. Sift confectioners' sugar over the top.

| Each serving provides: | | | |
|---|---|---|---|
| 206 | Calories | 40 g | Carbohydrate |
| 5 g | Protein | 121 mg | Sodium |
| 3 g | Fat | 136 mg | Cholesterol |

# Carrot Cake

*Makes 12 Servings*

| 1   | cup flour |
|-----|-----------|
| 1   | cup sugar |
| ½   | teaspoon baking soda |
| 1   | teaspoon cinnamon |
|     | Pinch salt |
| ½   | cup oil |
| 2   | eggs |
| 2   | cups grated carrots |

Blend all ingredients and mix very well. Pour into a greased and floured 9-inch baking pan. Bake 25-30 minutes at 350°.

---

Each serving provides:

| 204  | Calories | 27 g   | Carbohydrate |
|------|----------|--------|--------------|
| 3 g  | Protein  | 64 mg  | Sodium |
| 10 g | Fat      | 46 mg  | Cholesterol |

# Very Special Carrot Cake

*Makes 16 Servings*

| | | | | |
|---|---|---|---|---|
| 1½ | cups vegetable oil | 2 | cups flour, sifted |
| 1½ | cups sugar | 2 | teaspoons baking soda |
| 3 | eggs, well beaten | 2 | teaspoons cinnamon |
| 1 | cup crushed pineapple | 1 | teaspoon salt |
| 2 | cups grated carrots | 2 | cups flaked coconut |
| 3 | teaspoons vanilla | 1 | cup chopped walnuts |

Combine oil, sugar, eggs, pineapple (with juice), carrots, and vanilla. Sift together dry ingredients: combine mixtures. Add coconut and nuts. Mix batter well and pour into a 9 × 13-inch greased and floured pan. Bake 40-45 minutes at 350°.

# Topping

| | |
|---|---|
| ¼ | cup milk-free margarine |
| 1½ | cups confectioners' sugar |
| 1 | teaspoon vanilla |
| 1 | tablespoon milk substitute |

Blend margarine, sugar, and vanilla. Add milk substitute a little at a time to get the proper consistency. Spread on top of cooked carrot cake.

---

Each serving provides:

| 507 | Calories | 52 g | Carbohydrate |
|---|---|---|---|
| 5 g | Protein | 318 mg | Sodium |
| 32 g | Fat | 52 mg | Cholesterol |

# Apple-Nut Cake

*Makes 12 Servings*

3   cups flour

2   cups sugar

1   cup vegetable oil

4   eggs

¼   cup orange juice

1   tablespoon baking powder

1   teaspoon salt

1   cup coarsely chopped walnuts or pecans

5   medium baking apples

2   teaspoons cinnamon

5   tablespoons sugar

In a large mixing bowl combine flour, sugar, oil, eggs, orange juice, baking powder, and salt. With an electric mixer, beat until smooth. Stir in nuts. Peel and core apples. Cut into ½-inch pieces, letting them fall directly into a bowl. Add cinnamon and sugar. Toss. Add apples to batter. Grease and flour a 10-inch tube pan. Pour batter into pan. Bake in a preheated 350° oven about 1½ hours. Cool upright in pan.

|  | Each serving provides: | | |
|---|---|---|---|
| 548 | Calories | 73 g | Carbohydrate |
| 7 g | Protein | 315 mg | Sodium |
| 27 g | Fat | 91 mg | Cholesterol |

# Hot Fudge-Pudding Cake

*Makes 8 Servings*

| | |
|---|---|
| 1½ | cups sugar (divided into one cup and ½ cup) |
| 1 | cup flour |
| 7 | tablespoons cocoa powder (divided into 3 tablespoons and 4 tablespoons) |
| 2 | teaspoons baking powder |
| ¼ | teaspoon salt |
| ½ | cup milk substitute |
| ⅓ | cup margarine, melted |
| 2 | teaspoons vanilla |
| ½ | cup lightly packed brown sugar |
| 1½ | cups hot water |

Heat oven to 350°. In a medium mixing bowl, combine 1 cup sugar, flour, 3 tablespoons cocoa, baking powder, and salt. Blend in milk substitute, melted margarine, and vanilla. Beat until smooth. Pour batter into an 8-inch or 9-inch square pan. In a small bowl, combine remaining ½ cup sugar, brown sugar, and remaining 4 tablespoons cocoa powder. Sprinkle evenly over batter. Pour hot water over the top, but do not stir. Bake 40 minutes or until the center is almost set. Let stand 15 minutes. Spoon into dessert dishes, spooning sauce from the bottom of the pan over the top.

| Each serving provides: | | | |
|---|---|---|---|
| 357 | Calories | 67 g | Carbohydrate |
| 3 g | Protein | 279 mg | Sodium |
| 10 g | Fat | 00 mg | Cholesterol |

# Jiffy Strawberry Cake

*Makes 12 Servings*

1   box milk-free white cake mix
1   tablespoon flour
1   small box strawberry gelatin
¾   cup vegetable oil
½   cup water
3   eggs, well beaten
1   cup drained, cut up, fresh strawberries

Mix cake mix, flour, and gelatin. Combine oil and water and add to cake mixture. Add eggs and berries, alternately. Beat well. Pour batter in a 9 × 13-inch greased and floured pan. Bake 35-40 minutes at 350°.

| Each serving provides: | | | |
|---|---|---|---|
| 363 | Calories | 44 g | Carbohydrate |
| 4 g | Protein | 291 mg | Sodium |
| 19 g | Fat | 69 mg | Cholesterol |

# Old-Fashioned Jelly Roll

*Makes 12 Servings*

5   eggs, separated
1   cup sugar
1   tablespoon lemon juice
2   tablespoons lemon rind, grated
1   cup flour
1   cup jelly
    Confectioners' sugar

In a large bowl, beat egg yolks well. Add sugar and beat. Add juice and rind. In a small bowl, beat egg whites until stiff. Add flour and egg white alternately to batter, beating well. Pour into a jelly roll pan lined with waxed paper. Bake at 375° for 12-15 minutes. Turn out on a damp towel. Trim off the crusty edges and spread with jelly. Roll up and cool. Sprinkle with confectioners' sugar and slice.

| Each serving provides: | | | |
|---|---|---|---|
| 105 | Calories | 44 g | Carbohydrate |
| 4 g | Protein | 34 mg | Sodium |
| 2 g | Fat | 114 mg | Cholesterol |

# Mini Yellow Cake

*Makes 8 Servings*

½     cup milk-free margarine, softened
1½    cups sifted flour
¾     cup sugar
2½    teaspoons baking powder
½     teaspoon salt
1     egg
¾     cup water
1½    teaspoons vanilla

In a large bowl, blend margarine, flour, sugar, baking powder, and salt. Add egg and ½ the water and mix until just moist. Beat at medium speed until well blended. Add the rest of the water and vanilla. Beat again. Bake for 25 minutes at 375° in a greased and floured 9-inch square baking pan.

| Each serving provides: | | | |
|---|---|---|---|
| 266 | Calories | 36 g | Carbohydrate |
| 3 g | Protein | 413 mg | Sodium |
| 12 g | Fat | 34 mg | Cholesterol |

# Quick Pear Coffee Cake

*Makes 16 Servings (2-inch square piece per serving)*

| | |
|---|---|
| ¼ | cup salad oil |
| 1 | beaten egg (or substitute) |
| ½ | cup pear syrup (from can of pears) |
| 1½ | cups flour |
| ½ | cup sugar |
| 2 | teaspoons baking powder |
| ½ | teaspoon salt |
| 1 | 8-ounce can pears (in light syrup) |
| ½ | cup flour |
| ¼ | cup brown sugar |

Combine oil, egg, and pear syrup. Sift together flour, sugar, baking powder, and salt. Add to egg mixture and beat well. Pour into a greased 9-inch square baking pan. Cover with sliced pears. Mix flour and brown sugar. Sprinkle on top. Dot with margarine. Bake at 375° for about 25 minutes.

| Each serving provides: | | | |
|---|---|---|---|
| 137 | Calories | 24 g | Carbohydrate |
| 2 g | Protein | 128 mg | Sodium |
| 4 g | Fat | 17 mg | Cholesterol |

# Morning's Healthiest Cake

*Makes 6 Servings*

| | |
|---|---|
| 1½ | cups whole wheat flour |
| ½ | cup white flour |
| 1 | teaspoon salt |
| 1 | teaspoon baking powder |
| 1½ | tablespoons vegetable shortening |
| ¾ | cup water |
| 4 | tablespoons honey |
| ½ | cup bran cereal |
| ½ | teaspoon cinnamon |

Mix first four ingredients. Add shortening to dry mixture and mix till consistency of coarse crumb. Add water and 3 tablespoons honey. Blend together and pour into a greased 9-inch round pan. Drizzle 1 tablespoon honey over the top. Combine cereal and cinnamon and sprinkle over top. Bake about 12 minutes at 425°.

| Each serving provides: | | | |
|---|---|---|---|
| 237 | Calories | 45 g | Carbohydrate |
| 7 g | Protein | 440 mg | Sodium |
| 5 g | Fat | 00 mg | Cholesterol |

# Almond Pound Cake

*Makes 16 Servings*

| | |
|---|---|
| 1 | 2-ounce roll almond paste |
| 1 | cup sugar |
| 1 | cup milk-free margarine |
| 4 | eggs |
| ½ | cup milk substitute |
| 1 | teaspoon baking powder |
| 2 | cups sifted flour |

Combine almond paste, sugar, and margarine in a bowl. Mix with an electric mixer until light and fluffy. Continue beating and add eggs one at a time. Mix flour and baking powder; add to batter alternately with milk substitute. Beat until smooth. Grease and flour pans. (This cake is made in two 7½ × 3¾-inch loaf pans.) Fill pans ⅔ full. Bake at 350° about 50 minutes. May be prepared in a bundt pan and baked for 1 hour and 10 minutes.

---

Each serving provides:

| 288 | Calories | | 30 g | Carbohydrate |
|---|---|---|---|---|
| 5 g | Protein | | 185 mg | Sodium |
| 17 g | Fat | | 69 mg | Cholesterol |

# Apple Küchen

*Makes 12 Servings*

| | |
|---|---|
| 1¼ | cups sifted flour |
| ¼ | cup sugar |
| 1½ | teaspoons baking powder |
| ½ | teaspoon salt |
| ¼ | cup milk-free margarine |
| ¼ | cup milk substitute |
| 1 | egg, well beaten |
| 2 | teaspoons vanilla |
| 5 | cups thinly sliced tart apples |

In a medium bowl, mix flour with sugar, baking powder, and salt. Cut in margarine until the mixture resembles coarse crumbs. Add beaten egg, milk substitute, and vanilla. Stir with a fork until the mixture is smooth, about one full minute. Spread this batter evenly in a 9 × 13-inch pan that has been lightly greased. Arrange apple slices slightly overlapping one another in rows over batter. Sprinkle with topping. Bake at 400° about 35 minutes or until apple slices are tender. Remove to a wire rack. Brush with preserve mixture (see next page).

# Topping

| | |
|---|---|
| ¼ | cup sugar |
| 1 | teaspoon cinnamon |
| ¼ | cup milk-free margarine, melted |

Combine well.

*Recipe continues on page 252*

## Preserve Mixture

⅓   cup apricot preserves
1   tablespoon hot water

---

Each serving provides:

| 210 | Calories | 32 g | Carbohydrate |
|-----|----------|------|--------------|
| 2 g | Protein | 245 mg | Sodium |
| 9 g | Fat | 23 mg | Cholesterol |

---

## Berry Cake

*Makes 16 Servings*

Nonstick vegetable spray
1   pint berries of your choosing
1   prepared recipe cake batter
Confectioners' sugar

Spray a bundt cakepan with a nonstick vegetable spray. Pour in fresh or frozen berries (drain the juice first). Pour layer cake batter on top and bake according to directions. Invert, and berries have topped a decorative cake. Sprinkle with confectioners' sugar when cool.

---

Each serving provides:

| 208 | Calories | 29 g | Carbohydrate |
|-----|----------|------|--------------|
| 3 g | Protein | 216 mg | Sodium |
| 9 g | Fat | 51 mg | Cholesterol |

# Holiday Trifle

*Makes 10 Servings*

|       | Milk-free custard |
|-------|-------------------|
| 12    | ladyfingers, split |
| ¼     | cup seedless raspberry or strawberry jam |
| 2     | cups strawberries, or a combination of berries |
|       | Milk-free whipped cream |

# Milk-free Custard

| 1   | cup milk substitute | ½    | cup sugar |
|-----|---------------------|------|-----------|
| 1   | cup water           | 3    | tablespoons cornstarch |
| 4   | egg yolks           | 1½   | teaspoons vanilla |

Warm milk substitute and water, but do not boil. Beat the egg yolks in a large bowl and slowly add the sugar. Mix in cornstarch. Gradually add warm milk substitute mixture. Return to pan and stir over low heat until custard thickens. Do not allow to boil. Remove from heat, cool, and add vanilla. Cool 30 minutes.

Split ladyfingers and spread with jam. Arrange in a layer in a trifle bowl and spoon ⅓ of the fruit on top. Spoon ½ of the custard over this. Repeat with a layer of ladyfingers, fruit, and custard. Top with ladyfingers. Spread milk-free whipped cream over this. Garnish with fruit.

| Each serving provides: | | | |
|------|-----------|--------|-------------|
| 250  | Calories  | 34 g   | Carbohydrate |
| 3 g  | Protein   | 49 mg  | Sodium      |
| 12 g | Fat       | 156 mg | Cholesterol |

# Fresh Fruit Torte

*Makes 8 Servings*

| | |
|---|---|
| 1 | stick milk-free margarine, softened |
| 1 | cup sugar |
| 2 | eggs |
| 2 | cups flour |
| 1 | teaspoon baking powder |
| 1 | teaspoon vanilla |
| 2 | tablespoons cinnamon and sugar mixture |
| 2 | plums |
| 2 | peaches |
| ½ | cup blueberries |
| 2 | nectarines |

Cream margarine and sugar. Beat in eggs. Add flour, baking powder, and vanilla. Mix well. Pour batter into a 9-inch round cake pan. Slice fruit and cover the batter with assorted fruits. Sprinkle with cinnamon and sugar. Bake at 350° about 1 hour.

---

Each serving provides:

| 391 | Calories | 63 g | Carbohydrate |
|---|---|---|---|
| 6 g | Protein | 206 mg | Sodium |
| 13 g | Fat | 69 mg | Cholesterol |

# Kiwi Flan

*Makes 8 Servings*

1    prepared 10-inch sponge cake layer
5    kiwi fruit, peeled and sliced
1    11-ounce can mandarin oranges, drained
¼    cup apricot preserves
1    tablespoon brandy

Arrange kiwi slices, slightly overlapping around outer edge of cake. Arrange a ring of orange slices. Repeat, ending with orange slices in the center. In a small saucepan, heat preserves and brandy. Stir until bubbly. Brush over fruit and chill until serving time.

| Each serving provides: | | | |
|---|---|---|---|
| 369 | Calories | 75 g | Carbohydrate |
| 8g | Protein | 153 mg | Sodium |
| 5 g | Fat | 206 mg | Cholesterol |

# Egg-Free Chocolate Frosting

3     cups confectioners' sugar

¾     cup cocoa powder

⅛     teaspoon salt

2     teaspoons vanilla

⅓     cup milk-free margarine, softened

5     tablespoons milk substitute

Combine sugar, cocoa, salt, vanilla, and margarine, beating well. Slowly add milk substitute until frosting is of spreading consistency. Add additional milk substitute if necessary. Makes enough to frost a 9-inch layer cake.

---

Each serving provides:

| 140 | Calories | | 25 g | Carbohydrate |
|---|---|---|---|---|
| .08 g | Protein | | 66 mg | Sodium |
| 5 g | Fat | | 00 mg | Cholesterol |

# Creamy Chocolate Frosting

½   cup milk-free margarine, softened
2    cups confectioners' sugar
1    egg yolk
⅓   cup cocoa powder

Cream margarine and sugar until fluffy. Add egg yolk and beat; then beat in cocoa powder. If frosting is too thick, add a little warm water. Makes enough to frost a 9-inch layer cake.

| Each serving provides: | | | |
|---|---|---|---|
| 113 | Calories | 16 g | Carbohydrate |
| .04 g | Protein | 67 mg | Sodium |
| 6 g | Fat | 00 mg | Cholesterol |

# Lemon Frosting

½   cup milk-free margarine, softened
3    cups confectioners' sugar
2    tablespoons water
2    tablespoons lemon juice
1    tablespoon lemon rind, grated

Cream margarine and add remaining ingredients, beating until fluffy. Makes enough to frost a 9-inch layer cake.

| Each serving provides: | | | |
|---|---|---|---|
| 138 | Calories | 23 g | Carbohydrate |
| .06 g | Protein | 67 mg | Sodium |
| 6 g | Fat | 00 mg | Cholesterol |

# Peppermint Frosting

| | |
|---|---|
| 2 | egg whites |
| ¼ | teaspoon cream of tartar |
| ¼ | teaspoon salt |
| ¼ | cup sugar |
| ¾ | cup light corn syrup |
| 1¼ | teaspoons vanilla |
| ¼ | teaspoon peppermint extract |
| 2 | drops green food coloring |

In a small bowl, blend at high speed egg whites, cream of tartar, and salt until soft peaks form. Gradually beat in sugar until glossy. Gradually beat in corn syrup and vanilla. Add peppermint extract and blend well. Beat until stiff peaks form, about 6 minutes. Blend in food coloring.

Each serving provides:

| 60 | Calories | 15 g | Carbohydrate |
|---|---|---|---|
| .4 g | Protein | 50 mg | Sodium |
| 00 g | Fat | 00 mg | Cholesterol |

# Banana Frosting

| 2 | tablespoons milk-free margarine, softened |
| 1/4 | cup banana, mashed |
| 1/4 | teaspoon lemon juice |
| 1 1/4 | cups confectioners' sugar |

Combine ingredients and beat until smooth. Makes enough to frost a 9-inch layer cake.

Each serving provides:

| 59 | Calories | 12 g | Carbohydrate |
| .06 g | Protein | 17 mg | Sodium |
| 1.4 g | Fat | 00 mg | Cholesterol |

# Mocha Frosting

| 1/2 | cup milk-free margarine |
| 2 | cups confectioners' sugar |
| 1/2 | cup cocoa powder |
| 3 | tablespoons instant coffee |

Cream margarine and sugar until fluffy. Add cocoa powder and instant coffee. Beat until thick. Makes enough to frost a 9-inch layer cake.

Each serving provides:

| 117 | Calories | 17 g | Carbohydrate |
| .56 g | Protein | 67 mg | Sodium |
| 6 g | Fat | 00 mg | Cholesterol |

# Seven-Minute Icing

| | |
|---|---|
| 2 | egg whites |
| 1½ | cups sugar |
| ⅛ | teaspoon salt |
| ¼ | teaspoon cream of tartar |
| ½ | cup water |
| 1 | teaspoon lemon juice |

Combine egg whites, sugar, salt, cream of tartar, and water in top of a double boiler. Beat until well mixed. Beat for 7 minutes or until the icing stands in firm peaks. Remove from water and cool. Add lemon juice. Spread on cake.

---

Each serving provides:

| 74 | Calories | 19 g | Carbohydrate |
|---|---|---|---|
| .4 g | Protein | 24 mg | Sodium |
| 00 g | Fat | 00 mg | Cholesterol |

# Chocolate Glaze

3     tablespoons cocoa powder
3½   tablespoons melted milk-free margarine
1½   cups confectioners' sugar
1     teaspoon vanilla
3     tablespoons boiling water

Mix cocoa powder and margarine in saucepan and stir constantly over low heat until well blended. Stir in sugar and vanilla until crumbly. Add 1 teaspoon of water at a time until glaze pours well. Add more water if necessary. Pour quickly over the top of a cake or spread evenly. Makes enough to glaze a 9-inch layer cake.

---

Each serving provides:

| | | | |
|---|---|---|---|
| 69 | Calories | 12 g | Carbohydrate |
| .18 g | Protein | 29 mg | Sodium |
| 3 g | Fat | 00 mg | Cholesterol |

# White Glaze

1    tablespoon milk-free margarine, softened
½    teaspoon vanilla
     Dash salt
1    cup confectioners' sugar
2    tablespoons water

Place margarine, vanilla, and salt in a bowl. Add sugar and water alternately, beating after each addition until smooth. Add more water or sugar if needed for consistency.

| Each serving provides: | | | |
|---|---|---|---|
| 36 | Calories | 8 g | Carbohydrate |
| 0 g | Protein | 17 mg | Sodium |
| .7 g | Fat | 00 mg | Cholesterol |

# Puddings, Pies, and Tarts

## Plain Pastry

1½    cups sifted flour
½     teaspoon salt
½     cup solid shortening or milk-free margarine
5     tablespoons ice-cold water

Sift together flour and salt and cut in half the shortening until mixture is crumbly. Cut in remaining shortening. Do not overmix. Add 1 tablespoon water and gently toss. Repeat this until the mixture forms a ball. Flatten on a floured surface and roll to ⅛-inch thickness. Fit into a pie plate and prick. Bake at 425° for 10-12 minutes. Cool and fill. Makes one 9-inch pie crust or 4-6 tart shells.

| Each serving provides: | | | |
|---|---|---|---|
| 192 | Calories | 16 g | Carbohydrate |
| 2 g | Protein | 137 mg | Sodium |
| 13 g | Fat | 00 mg | Cholesterol |

# Graham Cracker Crust

1¼    cups graham crackers, crushed
3     tablespoons sugar
6     tablespoons melted milk-free margarine

Mix graham cracker crumbs with sugar. Stir into melted margarine and mix well. Press firmly onto bottom and sides of a 9-inch pie pan. Either chill 45 to 60 minutes or bake at 375° for about 6 minutes. Cool before filling. Yields one 9-inch pie crust.

| Each serving provides: | | | |
|---|---|---|---|
| 170 | Calories | 19 g | Carbohydrate |
| 1 g | Protein | 213 mg | Sodium |
| 10 g | Fat | 00 mg | Cholesterol |

# Chocolate-Nut Crust

3     ounces semi-sweet chocolate bits
2     tablespoons milk-free margarine
1¼    cups whole blanched almonds, toasted and finely chopped

Melt chocolate and margarine over low heat in a saucepan. Add chopped almonds. Stir until mixture is well blended. Refrigerate for 30 minutes. Spoon mixture into a greased 9-inch pie plate and press firmly. Refrigerate for 2 hours before filling.

| Each serving provides: | | | |
|---|---|---|---|
| 212 | Calories | 10 g | Carbohydrate |
| 5 g | Protein | 36 mg | Sodium |
| 19 g | Fat | 00 mg | Cholesterol |

# Meringue Pie Shell

1    cup sugar
½    teaspoon cream of tartar
4    egg whites
½    teaspoon salt

In a small bowl, sift sugar with cream of tartar. Set aside. In a large bowl, beat egg whites with salt until soft peaks form. Gradually add sugar mixture 2 tablespoons at a time. Beat after each addition. When all the sugar has dissolved and all the sugar/cream of tartar mixture has been added, beat at high speed for 10 minutes. Meringue should be stiff and glossy. Spoon into a greased 9-inch pie plate. Build up the sides to form a pie shell and smooth out. Preheat oven to 275°. Place the pie shell in the oven and immediately turn the heat down to 250°. Bake for 1½ hours. Turn the heat off, set the door ajar, and let the shell dry out in the oven for 1 hour. Remove and set to cool. Fill as desired.

|  | Each serving provides: | | |
|---|---|---|---|
| 104 | Calories | 25 g | Carbohydrate |
| 2 g | Protein | 162 mg | Sodium |
| 00 g | Fat | 00 mg | Cholesterol |

# Filbert Meringue Tarts

*Makes 8 Servings*

2     egg whites
½     cup sugar
½     cup finely chopped filberts
1     recipe Basic Vanilla Ice Cream

Beat egg whites to soft peaks. Gradually add sugar, beating until very stiff peaks form and sugar is dissolved. Fold in chopped nuts and blend well. Make six shells, in the following manner:

Cover cookie sheet with waxed paper. Using about ⅓ cup of meringue for each, spread meringue in a circle shape about 3 inches in diameter. Using the back of a spoon, pat out a shell area in the center. Bake at 275° for 1 hour. Remove from heat; cool thoroughly and fill with ice cream at serving time.

---

Each serving provides:

| 237 | Calories | 30 g | Carbohydrate |
|---|---|---|---|
| 3 g | Protein | 42 mg | Sodium |
| 13 g | Fat | 34 mg | Cholesterol |

# French Apple Flan

*Makes 8 Servings*

2       9-inch pastry shells, uncooked
2½      tablespoons flour
½       cup sugar
1       tablespoon water/1 tablespoon sugar mixture
3       large tart apples, thinly sliced

Place 1 pie shell in a greased flan pan. Layer apples around the shell. Mix flour and sugar. Sprinkle over apples. Cover with second pie crust. Press edges together. Brush top of crust with water and sugar mixture to glaze. Bake 40 minutes at 350°. Serve warm or at room temperature.

| Each serving provides: | | | |
|---|---|---|---|
| 478 | Calories | 57 g | Carbohydrate |
| 5 g | Protein | 274 mg | Sodium |
| 26 g | Fat | 00 mg | Cholesterol |

# Mom's Apple Pie

*Makes 8 Servings*

6-8   large Northern Spy apples (peeled and cored)
1      cup sugar
2      teaspoons cinnamon
2      tablespoons flour
2      9-inch plain pastry pie crusts, unbaked
3      tablespoons milk-free margarine

Thinly slice apples and mix with sugar, cinnamon, and flour. Fill an unbaked pastry shell and dot filling with margarine. Cover with the top crust, seal, and slit. Bake at 400° for about 1 hour.

| Each serving provides: | | | |
|---|---|---|---|
| 600 | Calories | 79 g | Carbohydrate |
| 5 g | Protein | 325 mg | Sodium |
| 31 g | Fat | 00 mg | Cholesterol |

# Strawberry-Rhubarb Pie

*Makes 8 Servings*

| | |
|---|---|
| 1 | pound frozen rhubarb, thawed and drained |
| 1 | pint strawberries, hulled and halved |
| 3 | tablespoons cornstarch |
| 3 | tablespoons lemon juice |
| ½ | teaspoon cinnamon |
| 1 | cup sugar |
| | Prepared 9-inch pie shell, unbaked |
| ¼ | cup strawberry preserves, heated |

In a small bowl, mix sugar, cornstarch, lemon juice, and cinnamon and blend well. Toss into rhubarb and strawberries. Let stand 15 minutes. Spoon this filling into pie shell. Bake at 450° for 10 minutes. Reduce heat to 350° and bake 35-40 minutes until crust is golden. Cool at least 30 minutes. Brush filling with heated strawberry preserves. Sprinkle with powdered sugar.

| Each serving provides: | | | |
|---|---|---|---|
| 352 | Calories | 57 g | Carbohydrate |
| 3 g | Protein | 141 mg | Sodium |
| 13 g | Fat | 00 mg | Cholesterol |

# Tofu Cheesecake

*Makes 8 Servings*

24    ounces tofu, drained
½     cup sugar
1     tablespoon vanilla
2     tablespoons vegetable oil
1     tablespoon lemon juice
⅛     teaspoon cinnamon
1     tablespoon grated lemon peel
1     9-inch graham cracker crust

Combine all filling ingredients in a blender and mix until smooth. Pour into prepared pie crust and bake at 350° for about 40 minutes. Top with fruit if desired (½ can cherry pie filling or ½ can blueberry pie filling).

| | Each serving provides: | | |
|---|---|---|---|
| 319 | Calories | 33 g | Carbohydrate |
| 8 g | Protein | 219 mg | Sodium |
| 17 g | Fat | 00 mg | Cholesterol |

# Lemon Meringue Pie

*Makes 8 Servings*

| | |
|---|---|
| 1¼ | cups sugar |
| 3 | tablespoons cornstarch |
| 3 | tablespoons flour |
| 1½ | cups hot water |
| 3 | eggs (separated) |
| 2 | tablespoons milk-free margarine |
| 1 | teaspoon lemon peel, grated |
| ⅓ | cup lemon juice |
| 1 | 9-inch pie crust (plain or graham cracker) |

Heat sugar, cornstarch, and flour in a saucepan over medium heat. Gradually add hot water, stirring constantly until mixture boils. Reduce heat and cook 5-6 minutes longer. Set aside. Beat egg yolks slightly and add a little of the hot mixture. Pour all the egg mixture into saucepan and bring to a boil. Add margarine and lemon peel. Then add lemon juice very slowly, mixing well. Pour into a pie shell. Top with meringue and bake at 350° for 10-15 minutes, or until meringue is lightly browned.

# Meringue

| | | | |
|---|---|---|---|
| 3 | egg whites | ¼ | teaspoon cream of tartar |
| ½ | teaspoon vanilla | 5 | tablespoons sugar |

Mix egg whites, vanilla, and cream of tartar. Beat until soft peaks form. Gradually add sugar and continue beating until meringue is stiff and shiny.

| Each serving provides: | | | |
|---|---|---|---|
| 428 | Calories | 61 g | Carbohydrate |
| 6 g | Protein | 218 mg | Sodium |
| 18 g | Fat | 103 mg | Cholesterol |

# Lemon Pie

*Makes 8 Servings*

2      eggs
¾      cup sugar
1      tablespoon potato starch
1      cup water
1      teaspoon oil
       Juice of one lemon
1      prepared 9-inch pie shell

In a small bowl, beat eggs well. Mix together sugar and
potato starch. Slowly add to beaten egg mixture. In another
bowl, combine water, oil, and lemon juice. Add this to egg
mixture. Cook in top of double boiler until thick. Cool thoroughly. Fill the prepared pie shell.

---

| Each serving provides: | | | |
|---|---|---|---|
| 293 | Calories | 36 g | Carbohydrate |
| 4 g | Protein | 155 mg | Sodium |
| 15 g | Fat | 69 mg | Cholesterol |

# Tofu Lemon Pie

*Makes 8 Servings*

| | |
|---|---|
| 1 | package lemon gelatin |
| 2 | cups boiling water |
| 1½ | cups cold water |
| 1 | 14½-ounce package soft tofu |
| 3 | tablespoons lemon juice |
| 2 | teaspoons grated lemon peel |
| 1 | graham cracker crust, 9- or 10-inch |

Dissolve gelatin in boiling water. Add cold water and chill until consistency of egg whites. Place in blender with tofu and lemon juice. Blend well. Mix in lemon peel; pour into crust, and chill until firm. Serve topped with strawberries or other fresh fruit.

---

Each serving provides:

| 249 | Calories | 29 g | Carbohydrate |
|---|---|---|---|
| 7 g | Protein | 251 mg | Sodium |
| 12 g | Fat | 00 mg | Cholesterol |

---

# Daiquiri Pie

*Makes 8 Servings*

| | |
|---|---|
| 1⅓ | cups sugar |
| 1 | envelope unflavored gelatin |
| ¼ | teaspoon salt |
| ⅓ | cup fresh lime juice |
| ⅓ | cup water |
| 3 | separated eggs |
| ½ | teaspoon grated lime peel |
| 3 | drops green food coloring |
| ¼ | cup rum |
| ⅓ | cup sugar |
| 1 | 9-inch graham cracker pie crust |
| 1 | cup shredded coconut |

In a saucepan, combine 1 cup sugar, gelatin, and salt. Add lime juice and water. Beat egg yolks and stir into the gelatin mixture. Cook over low heat until gelatin dissolves, stirring constantly. Remove from heat; add lime peel and food coloring. Cool to room temperature and add rum. Chill until mixture is quite thick. Beat egg whites to soft peaks. Gradually add ⅓ cup sugar and continue to beat until mixture is stiff. Fold in gelatin mixture. Chill for about 30 minutes or until soft mounds are formed. Spoon into the graham cracker crust and chill at least 5 hours before serving. Top with coconut.

| Each serving provides: | | | |
|---|---|---|---|
| 424 | Calories | 65 g | Carbohydrate |
| 5 g | Protein | 331 mg | Sodium |
| 15 g | Fat | 103 mg | Cholesterol |

# Chocolate Cream Pie

*Makes 8 Servings*

| | |
|---|---|
| 1 | envelope unflavored gelatin |
| ¼ | cup cold water |
| 3 | eggs, separated |
| ½ | cup sugar |
| 1 | teaspoon vanilla |
| 2 | tablespoons milk-free margarine |
| 6 | tablespoons cocoa powder |
| ½ | cup water |
| 1 | tablespoon chocolate liqueur or rum |
| ½ | cup sugar |
| 1 | 9-inch graham cracker crust |

Soften gelatin in ¼ cup cold water and set aside. Beat egg yolks until thick; then beat in sugar and vanilla. In a small pan, over very low heat, melt margarine and add cocoa and ½ cup water. Stir until well blended. Add softened gelatin, stirring until dissolved. Beat chocolate mixture into egg yolks and add liqueur. Chill until almost set. Beat room-temperature egg whites until thick. Gradually add ½ cup sugar, beating until stiff. Fold a little egg white into chocolate mixture. Then, slowly fold chocolate mixture into egg whites. Pour into a cool shell. Refrigerate until firm.

| Each serving provides: | | | |
|---|---|---|---|
| 341 | Calories | 46 g | Carbohydrate |
| 5 g | Protein | 273 mg | Sodium |
| 16 g | Fat | 103 mg | Cholesterol |

# Strawberry Cream Pie

*Makes 8 Servings*

1   8-ounce container Rich's Richwhip
1   3-ounce package strawberry gelatin
1   cup fresh strawberries, sliced
1   9-inch graham cracker crust

Whip the non-dairy whipping cream according to package directions. Set in refrigerator. Make gelatin according to speed-set directions. When thickened, mix with whipped cream, beating well. Fold in strawberries and pour mixture into pie shell. Chill until firm.

| Each serving provides: | | | |
|---|---|---|---|
| 295 | Calories | 33 g | Carbohydrate |
| 2 g | Protein | 267 mg | Sodium |
| 18 g | Fat | 00 mg | Cholesterol |

# Pumpkin Mousse

*Makes 8 Servings*

1    envelope unflavored gelatin

⅓    cup cold water

¾    cup (1 can) pumpkin

½    cup brown sugar

2    teaspoons cinnamon

1    teaspoon ginger

½    teaspoon salt

2    eggs, separated

⅓    cup sugar
     Milk-free whipped cream
     Chopped pecans

In a small saucepan, mix unflavored gelatin with cold water. Stir over low heat until dissolved. Add pumpkin, sugar, cinnamon, ginger, salt, and beaten egg yolks. Cook over medium heat until thoroughly heated. Cool completely. Beat the egg whites with sugar until stiff. Fold into pumpkin mixture. Chill thoroughly. Serve with milk-free whipped cream and chopped pecans.

| Each serving provides: | | | |
|---|---|---|---|
| 116 | Calories | 24 g | Carbohydrate |
| 3 g | Protein | 160 mg | Sodium |
| 1 g | Fat | 69 mg | Cholesterol |

# Chocolate Mousse

*Makes 8 Servings*

½   cup milk-free margarine
¾   cup cocoa powder
5   tablespoons cold water
5   eggs, separated
1½  cups sugar

Melt margarine in saucepan and add cocoa powder and water. Blend and let mixture cool slightly. Beat egg yolks in a bowl. Add chocolate mixture. In a separate bowl, beat egg whites until stiff. Add sugar and beat again. Fold ¼ of the egg whites into the chocolate mixture. Add remaining egg whites a little at a time, blending very gently. Pour into a 9-inch glass bowl and refrigerate. Mousse will be ready in 1 hour.

| Each serving provides: | | | |
|---|---|---|---|
| 317 | Calories | 42 g | Carbohydrate |
| 5 g | Protein | 178 mg | Sodium |
| 16 g | Fat | 171 mg | Cholesterol |

# Chocolate Mousse Crêpes

*Makes 18 Servings*

1   recipe Chocolate Mousse
1   recipe crêpes
     Milk-free whipped cream

Prepare Chocolate Mousse recipe and refrigerate for at least 1
hour. During that time, prepare 1 recipe crêpes (or use crêpes
that have been prepared earlier). Place a dollop of mousse on a
crêpe. Fold in the sides and refrigerate. When ready to serve,
top with milk-free whipped cream.

Each serving provides:

| 245 | Calories | 29 g | Carbohydrate |
|---|---|---|---|
| 5 g | Protein | 244 mg | Sodium |
| 14 g | Fat | 122 mg | Cholesterol |

# Raspberry-Pineapple Pudding

*Makes 5 Servings*

1   cup unsweetened canned pineapple juice
1   envelope unflavored gelatin
1   8-ounce can unsweetened crushed pineapple
1   10-ounce package frozen raspberries, thawed

Put pineapple juice in a medium saucepan and sprinkle gelatin over it. Let soften about 5 minutes. Add the crushed pineapple and heat on low heat, stirring until the gelatin dissolves. Remove from heat. Add raspberries and syrup. Ladle into 6-ounce custard cups or individual molds. Chill to set.

| Each serving provides: | | | |
|---|---|---|---|
| 116 | Calories | 28 g | Carbohydrate |
| 2 g | Protein | 3 mg | Sodium |
| .13 g | Fat | 00 mg | Cholesterol |

# Carrot Pudding

*Makes 12 Servings (2½-inch piece per serving)*

½    cup milk-free margarine
¾    cup brown sugar
3     eggs, separated
1½   cups flour
1     tablespoon water
1     tablespoon cinnamon
½    teaspoon baking soda
½    teaspoon baking powder
1     teaspoon salt
3     cups grated carrots

*Recipe continued on page 281*

Cream margarine and sugar. Add egg yolks, flour, water, cinnamon, baking soda, baking powder, and salt. Blend thoroughly. Add carrots and blend. In a large bowl, beat egg whites until stiff. Gently fold carrot mixture into egg whites and fill a 9-inch square pan. Bake at 350° for 1 hour. Serve hot.

| Each serving provides: | | | |
|---|---|---|---|
| 210 | Calories | 29 g | Carbohydrate |
| 4 g | Protein | 356 mg | Sodium |
| 9 g | Fat | 69 mg | Cholesterol |

# Colonial Apple Custard

*Makes 4 Servings*

1    tablespoon melted milk-free margarine

1    cup applesauce

3    beaten eggs

¼    teaspoon salt

1    teaspoon vanilla

½    teaspoon nutmeg

Grease four custard cups. Combine remaining margarine, applesauce, eggs, salt, and vanilla extract. Pour into cups. Sprinkle with nutmeg. Bake at 350° about 30 minutes or until a knife comes out clean. Best served cold.

| Each serving provides: | | | |
|---|---|---|---|
| 138 | Calories | 14 g | Carbohydrate |
| 5 g | Protein | 222 mg | Sodium |
| 7 g | Fat | 206 mg | Cholesterol |

# Stone-Soup Tarts

3   eggs, beaten well
4   cups of any of the following:
    nuts
    raisins
    chopped dates
    coconut
    semi-sweet chocolate bits
    currants
    dried apricot pieces

Combine tart mixture. Fill paper baking cups about ⅔ full and set into a cupcake pan. Bake at 350° for 15-18 minutes. Let cool thoroughly.

# Cookies and Bars

## Chocolate-Peanut Butter Cookies

*Makes 12 Servings (3 cookies each serving)*

1     cup flour
½     teaspoon baking soda
⅓     cup melted milk-free margarine
⅓     cup sugar
⅓     cup firmly packed brown sugar
1     egg
1     teaspoon vanilla
½     cup chunky peanut butter
¼     cup milk-free chocolate syrup

In a small bowl, combine flour and soda. In a larger bowl, cream margarine and sugars until fluffy. Add egg and vanilla and beat well. Add peanut butter and chocolate syrup and beat well. Add the flour and blend slowly with a spoon. Drop by rounded teaspoons onto an ungreased cookie sheet. Bake at 375° for about 10 minutes. Let stand about a minute before removing from cookie sheet. Yield: 3 dozen.

| Each serving provides: | | | |
|---|---|---|---|
| 214 | Calories | 24 g | Carbohydrate |
| 5 g | Protein | 148 mg | Sodium |
| 11 g | Fat | 23 mg | Cholesterol |

# Peanut Butter-and-Jelly Cookies

*Makes 16 Servings (3 cookies each serving)*

½    cup milk-free margarine
½    cup creamy peanut butter
½    cup sugar
½    cup brown sugar
1    egg, beaten
½    teaspoon vanilla
1    cup flour
¾    teaspoon baking soda
¼    teaspoon salt
     Your favorite jelly

Cream margarine, peanut butter, and sugars until smooth. Add egg and vanilla. Sift together dry ingredients and blend into creamed mixture. Shape into 1-inch balls and place on an ungreased cookie sheet. Press each cookie with a fork. Drop a small round of jelly in the middle of each cookie. Bake at 375° for 10-12 minutes. Cool slightly before removing from pan. Makes about 4 dozen cookies.

---

Each serving provides:

| 233 | Calories | 33 g | Carbohydrate |
|-----|----------|------|--------------|
| 4 g | Protein | 187 mg | Sodium |
| 10 g | Fat | 17 mg | Cholesterol |

# Cinnamon Cookies

*Makes 20 Servings (3 cookies each serving)*

| | |
|---|---|
| 2¾ | cups sifted flour |
| 2 | teaspoons cream of tartar |
| ½ | teaspoon salt |
| 1 | cup milk-free margarine |
| 1⅓ | cups sugar |
| 2 | eggs, beaten |
| ¼ | cup cinnamon |
| ½ | cup sugar |

Sift together the first 4 ingredients and set aside. Cream margarine and sugar. Add eggs. Gradually add dry ingredients. Chill dough for 1 hour. Roll into 1-inch balls; then roll in a mixture of cinnamon and sugar. Place about 2 inches apart on an ungreased cookie sheet. Bake at 400° for approximately 8 minutes, or until lightly browned. Makes about 5 dozen cookies.

---

|  | Each serving provides: | | |
|---|---|---|---|
| 221 | Calories | 31 g | Carbohydrate |
| 2 g | Protein | 211 mg | Sodium |
| 10 g | Fat | 27 mg | Cholesterol |

# Poppyseed Cookies

*Makes 18 Servings (4 cookies each serving)*

3     eggs
1     cup sugar
¾     cup vegetable oil
¼     cup orange juice
¼     teaspoon salt
¼     cup poppyseeds
2     cups flour

Beat eggs until foamy. Beat in sugar, oil, orange juice, salt, and half the poppyseeds. Add flour and beat until well blended. Drop by half-teaspoons about 1 inch apart on an ungreased cookie sheet. Bake at 350° about 15-18 minutes. Remove from oven and immediately remove cookies from cookie sheet. Makes about 6 dozen.

| | Each serving provides: | | |
|---|---|---|---|
| 199 | Calories | 23 g | Carbohydrate |
| 3 g | Protein | 42 mg | Sodium |
| 11 g | Fat | 46 mg | Cholesterol |

# Strudel Cookies

*Makes 18 Servings (4 cookies each serving)*

| | |
|---|---|
| 1½ | cups flour |
| ½ | cup margarine |
| 3 | egg yolks, beaten |
| 1 | teaspoon lemon rind |
| 1 | tablespoon lemon juice |

Cut margarine into flour until crumbly. Stir in egg yolks, lemon rind, and lemon juice. Blend lightly with a fork to form a pastry dough. Form 24 walnut-sized balls and chill at least 4 hours or overnight. Prepare filling.

# Filling

| | |
|---|---|
| 3 | egg whites |
| ½ | cup sugar |
| 1 | cup ground walnuts |

Beat egg whites, adding sugar gradually to form meringue. Fold in ground walnuts and set aside.

Roll out each pastry ball until about 4 inches round. Spread with 2 tablespoons nut mixture. Roll up like a jelly roll and place seam side down on an ungreased cookie sheet. Bake at 350° about 15 minutes or until golden brown. Cool and slice diagonally into 3 pieces. Sprinkle with confectioners' sugar. Makes 6 dozen.

---

Each serving provides:

| 152 | Calories | 15 g | Carbohydrate |
|---|---|---|---|
| 3 g | Protein | 70 mg | Sodium |
| 9 g | Fat | 45 mg | Cholesterol |

# Jam Swirls

*Makes 6 Servings (2 rolls each serving)*

Prepare Quick and Easy Yeast Rolls. After kneading, roll dough into a rectangle shape 12 × 9-inches. Spread ⅓ cup jam to within ½ inch of edge. Roll up, beginning at the wide side. Pinch the edge of dough into roll to seal. Cut roll into twelve 1-inch slices, and arrange in pan. Continue as directed. Bake 15-17 minutes. Immediately remove from pan. While warm, drizzle with this glaze: ½ cup powdered sugar mixed with 1 tablespoon water.

|  |  |  |  |
|---|---|---|---|
| | **Each serving provides:** | | |
| 350 | Calories | 67 g | Carbohydrate |
| 7 g | Protein | 198 mg | Sodium |
| 6 g | Fat | 46 mg | Cholesterol |

# Sugar Cookies

*Makes 16 Servings (3 cookies each serving)*

| | |
|---|---|
| 2 | cups sifted flour |
| 1½ | teaspoons baking powder |
| ½ | teaspoon salt |
| ½ | cup milk-free margarine |
| ¾ | cup sugar |
| 1 | egg |
| 1 | teaspoon vanilla |
| 1 | tablespoon warm water |
| | Sugar |

Sift together the first 3 ingredients and set aside. In a large bowl, cream margarine and sugar. Add egg, vanilla, and water. Beat well. Add dry ingredients and blend well. Refrigerate for about 1 hour. Roll to ¼-inch thickness and shape with cookie cutters. Sprinkle with sugar. Bake on an ungreased cookie sheet at 375° for about 8 minutes. Makes about 4 dozen cookies.

| Each serving provides: | | | |
|---|---|---|---|
| 158 | Calories | 24 g | Carbohydrate |
| 2 g | Protein | 180 mg | Sodium |
| 6 g | Fat | 17 mg | Cholesterol |

# Rugalach

*Makes 16 Servings (3 cookies each serving)*

3    cups flour
½    pound milk-free margarine
3    egg yolks
1    cup milk substitute
1    tablespoon dry yeast (one package)

# Topping

½    cup chopped walnuts or pecans
¾    cup sugar
1    teaspoon cinnamon

Mix flour and margarine until well blended. Combine egg yolks and milk substitute. Add egg mixture to the flour mixture and blend well. Sprinkle yeast over the top and mix with hands. Divide dough into 6 parts, wrap each in foil and refrigerate for several hours. Roll each piece of dough into a circle on a floured board. Preheat the oven to 325°. Combine the last three ingredients and sprinkle this topping on each circle of dough on both sides. Cut each circle into 8 wedges like a pie. Roll up each wedge, starting at the inside end. Bake on greased cookie sheet for 25 minutes or until golden brown. Makes 48 pieces of pastry.

| Each serving provides: | | | |
|---|---|---|---|
| 281 | Calories | 29 g | Carbohydrate |
| 4 g | Protein | 148 mg | Sodium |
| 17 g | Fat | 51 mg | Cholesterol |

# Anise Biscuits

*Makes 16 Servings (2 slices each serving)*

| | |
|---|---|
| 4½ | cups flour |
| ½ | teaspoon salt |
| 4 | teaspoons baking powder |
| ½ | pound milk-free margarine |
| 1½ | cups sugar |
| 5 | eggs (beat four, reserve; beat one, reserve) |
| 2 | ounces anise extract |

Sift flour, salt, and baking powder in a large mixing bowl. Cut in margarine. Add sugar, 4 eggs, and extract. Mix well. Shape into small loaves about 2 inches wide and 8 inches long. Brush tops with a beaten egg and bake on a greased cookie sheet at 350° about 30 minutes. Cool on a wire rack at least 20 minutes. Cut into thin slices and put back on cookie sheet to toast until lightly browned.

| Each serving provides: | | | |
|---|---|---|---|
| 341 | Calories | 46 g | Carbohydrate |
| 6 g | Protein | 331 mg | Sodium |
| 14 g | Fat | 86 mg | Cholesterol |

# Clara's Mandel Bread

*Makes 18 Servings (2 slices each serving)*

| | |
|---|---|
| 1 | cup vegetable oil |
| 1 | cup sugar |
| 4 | eggs |
| ¼ | cup orange juice |
| 3½ | cups flour |
| 2 | heaping teaspoons baking powder |
| ¾ | cup chopped nuts |
| 6 | ounces semi-sweet chocolate bits |
| 1 | cup raisins |
| 1 | cup cinnamon/sugar mixture |

Blend oil and sugar. Add eggs, juice, flour, baking powder, nuts, and chips. Mix until well blended. With wet hands, form loaves of dough about 4 inches wide and 12 inches long. Bake at 325° for 30 minutes. Cool and slice into 1-inch diagonals. Put back on a cookie sheet on its side; sprinkle with cinnamon and sugar. Toast at 325° for 5 minutes. Turn over. Repeat.

---

Each serving provides:

| 404 | Calories | 54 g | Carbohydrate |
|---|---|---|---|
| 6 g | Protein | 71 mg | Sodium |
| 20 g | Fat | 61 mg | Cholesterol |

# Apricot Bars

*Makes 24 Servings (1 2-inch bar per person)*

| | |
|---|---|
| 1½ | cups quick oats |
| 1½ | cups flour |
| 1¾ | cups firmly packed brown sugar |
| 1 | cup softened milk-free margarine |
| ½ | cup wheat germ |
| ½ | teaspoon baking soda |
| ¼ | teaspoon salt |
| 1 | 15.5-ounce jar of apricot preserves |

Preheat oven to 400°. In a large bowl, mix oats, flour, brown sugar, margarine, wheat germ, baking soda, and salt with an electric mixer. Beat on low until mixture is crumbly. Reserve 2 cups of this mixture and set aside. Press remainder in a greased 9 × 13-inch pan and bake for 8-10 minutes, or until lightly brown. Remove from oven and let cool slightly. Spread with apricot preserves, bringing the filling to within ¼ inch of the sides. Sprinkle evenly with the remaining crumb mixture, pressing lightly with the back of a spoon. Continue baking 25-30 minutes or until golden brown. Cool and cut.

| Each serving provides: | | | |
|---|---|---|---|
| 219 | Calories | 35 g | Carbohydrate |
| 3 g | Protein | 135 mg | Sodium |
| 9 g | Fat | 00 mg | Cholesterol |

# Peanut Butter-Chocolate Bars

*Makes 24 Servings (1 2-inch bar per serving)*

1      12-ounce jar crunchy peanut butter
2      cups graham cracker crumbs
¾      cup melted milk-free margarine
1      cup confectioners' sugar
1      12-ounce bag semi-sweet chocolate bits

Mix together peanut butter, graham cracker crumbs, margarine, and sugar. Press into an ungreased 13 × 9-inch pan. Bake at 375° for 5-7 minutes. Melt chocolate chips and pour on top of baked mixture. Spread evenly and let cool. Refrigerate until completely chilled and cut into squares. Makes about 24 bars.

---

Each serving provides:

| 266  | Calories | 22 g   | Carbohydrate |
|------|----------|--------|--------------|
| 6 g  | Protein  | 185 mg | Sodium       |
| 19 g | Fat      | 00 mg  | Cholesterol  |

# Holiday Bars

*Makes 24 Servings (3 pieces each serving)*

1   cup milk-free margarine, softened
1   egg
2   tablespoons milk substitute
1   teaspoon vanilla
1   cup confectioners' sugar
2   cups candied cherries
1   cup pecan halves

In a large mixing bowl, combine all ingredients except cherries and nuts. Blend well. Gently stir in cherries and nuts. Mix thoroughly. Shape dough into two 10-inch rolls. Wrap and chill at least 2 hours. Cut into ¼-inch slices. Place on an ungreased baking sheet. Bake 7-10 minutes at 400°. Makes about 6 dozen.

| Each serving provides: | | | |
|---|---|---|---|
| 165 | Calories | 17 g | Carbohydrate |
| .74 g | Protein | 93 mg | Sodium |
| 11 g | Fat | 11 mg | Cholesterol |

# Lemon Squares

*Makes 24 Servings (1 2-inch square per serving)*

2       cups flour
1       cup milk-free margarine
½       cup confectioners' sugar
4       eggs, beaten
2       cups sugar
½       cup lemon juice
¼       cup flour
½       teaspoon baking powder
        Confectioners' sugar

Combine flour, margarine, and confectioners' sugar to form crust. Press into a 9 × 13-inch pan and bake at 350° for 20 minutes. Mix together the eggs, sugar, lemon juice, flour, and baking powder. Pour over the baked crust. Bake about 25 minutes at 350°. Sprinkle with confectioners' sugar while still warm. Cut into squares.

| Each serving provides: | | | |
|---|---|---|---|
| 200 | Calories | 29 g | Carbohydrate |
| 3 g | Protein | 111 mg | Sodium |
| 9 g | Fat | 46 mg | Cholesterol |

# Pecan Brownies

*Makes 24 Servings (1 2-inch square per serving)*

| | |
|---|---|
| 2½ | cups flour |
| 1 | pound light-brown sugar |
| 1 | cup milk-free margarine, cut into ½-inch pieces |
| 2 | eggs at room temperature |
| 1 | teaspoon vanilla |
| 1½ | teaspoons baking powder |
| 1 | cup chopped pecans |

Combine 1¼ cups flour with ⅓ cup brown sugar in a medium bowl. Cut in ½ cup margarine until mixture resembles coarse meal. Press into the bottom of a lightly greased 9 × 13-inch baking pan. Bake at 350° about 15 minutes. Meantime, cook remaining brown sugar in a medium saucepan over low heat until sugar dissolves. Beat eggs in a large bowl with an electric mixer until pale yellow and a ribbon forms when beaters are lifted. Gradually beat in brown sugar mixture. Stir in vanilla, blending thoroughly. Sift remaining 1¼ cups flour with 1½ teaspoons baking powder and salt into brown sugar mixture. Blend well. Stir in pecans. Spread this mixture over baked crust. Bake an additional 25 minutes. Cool in the pan on a wire rack. Cut into squares. Wrap brownies tightly in plastic wrap and store in a covered container.

| Each serving provides: | | | |
|---|---|---|---|
| 447 | Calories | 58 g | Carbohydrate |
| 5 g | Protein | 255 mg | Sodium |
| 22 g | Fat | 46 mg | Cholesterol |

# Best-Ever Brownies

*Makes 16 Brownies*

½   cup milk-free margarine
1   cup plus 2 tablespoons sugar
2   eggs
1   teaspoon vanilla
¾   cup flour
¼   teaspoon salt
½   teaspoon baking powder
½   cup cocoa powder
¾   cup walnuts, chopped (optional)
    Confectioners' sugar (optional)

Cream margarine and sugar. Add eggs and vanilla and mix well. Sift together flour, salt, and baking powder and add to creamed mixture. Blend in cocoa powder and add chopped nuts. Spread mixture into a greased 9-inch square pan and bake at 350° for 35 minutes. When cool, top with a dusting of confectioners' sugar.

| Each serving provides: | | | |
|---|---|---|---|
| 145 | Calories | 20 g | Carbohydrate |
| 2 g | Protein | 123 mg | Sodium |
| 7 g | Fat | 35 mg | Cholesterol |

# Egg Yolk-Free Hazelnut Cookies

*Makes 8 Servings (3 cookies each serving)*

1¼    cups chopped hazelnuts (about ⅓ pound)
⅔     cup sugar
3      tablespoons flour
1      tablespoon cornstarch
       Pinch salt
3      tablespoons milk-free margarine, melted and cooled
1      teaspoon vanilla
1      teaspoon cinnamon
3      egg whites

Combine hazelnuts, sugar, flour, cornstarch, and salt in a large bowl. Blend margarine with vanilla and cinnamon in a small bowl. Add margarine mixture to nut mixture and blend well. Add egg whites and mix until smooth. Chill 30 minutes. Preheat oven to 400°. Line a baking sheet with foil. Drop batter onto baking sheet by ½ teaspoons, spacing about 2 inches apart. Dip a small metal spatula into cold water. Spread cookies to about 1¼ inches, moistening the spatula for each cookie. Bake about 7-8 minutes or until cookies are a deep golden brown. Cool on a wire rack. Makes about two dozen.

| Each serving provides: | | | |
|---|---|---|---|
| 244 | Calories | 23 g | Carbohydrate |
| 4 g | Protein | 86 mg | Sodium |
| 16 g | Fat | 00 mg | Cholesterol |

# Egg-Free Scottish Shortbread

*Makes 12 Servings (3 cookies each serving)*

| | |
|---|---|
| 1 | cup milk-free margarine |
| ¾ | cup sugar |
| 1-½ | cups flour |
| ½ | teaspoon baking soda |
| 1½ | teaspoons vanilla |
| 1 | teaspoon vinegar |
| ½ | cup chopped pecans |
| ½ | cup coconut flakes |

In a medium-sized bowl, cream margarine and sugar. Stir in flour and baking soda. Beat in vanilla, vinegar, pecans, and coconut. Drop by teaspoonfuls onto an ungreased cookie sheet. Bake at 350° about 12-15 minutes. Makes 3 dozen.

---

Each serving provides:

| 287 | Calories | 27 g | Carbohydrate |
|---|---|---|---|
| 2 g | Protein | 221 mg | Sodium |
| 19 g | Fat | 00 mg | Cholesterol |

# Egg-Free Meltaways

*Makes 8 Servings (3 cookies each serving)*

| | |
|---|---|
| 1 | cup flour |
| ½ | cup cornstarch |
| ½ | cup confectioners' sugar |
| 1½ | cups milk-free margarine, cut into 16 pats |

In a food processor with a steel blade, combine flour, cornstarch, and sugar. Spread pats of margarine over dry mixture. Process until blended. Using about 1 tablespoon for each, shape into balls and place on an ungreased cookie sheet, about 1½ inches apart. Flatten in a criss-cross fashion with a floured fork. Bake at 300° until edges are lightly browned, about 20 minutes. Makes about 2 dozen cookies.

---

Each serving provides:

| 420 | Calories | 27 g | Carbohydrate |
|---|---|---|---|
| 2 g | Protein | 402 mg | Sodium |
| 34 g | Fat | 00 mg | Cholesterol |

# Egg-Free Bonbon Cookies

*Makes 12 Servings (3 cookies each serving)*

| | |
|---|---|
| 1½ | cups milk-free margarine, softened |
| 1½ | cups confectioners' sugar |
| 2 | tablespoons vanilla |
| 3 | cups flour |
| | Maraschino cherries |

Cream margarine thoroughly. Add sugar and vanilla and continue beating until mixture is light and fluffy. Blend in flour. For each cookie, shape one level tablespoon of dough around a cherry. Form into a ball and place balls 1 inch apart on an ungreased cookie sheet. Bake at 350° for about 12-15 minutes.

---

Each serving provides:

| | | | |
|---|---|---|---|
| 391 | Calories | 42 g | Carbohydrate |
| 4 g | Protein | 268 mg | Sodium |
| 23 g | Fat | 00 mg | Cholesterol |

# Egg-Free Vienna Crescents

*Makes 16 Servings (3 cookies each serving)*

1¾   cups milk-free margarine

⅔    cup sugar

3½   cups flour

1     cup finely chopped almonds

      Confectioners' sugar

Cream margarine thoroughly. Add sugar gradually and continue beating until mixture is light and fluffy. Add flour gradually and beat until thoroughly mixed. Blend in chopped almonds. Place dough in waxed paper and chill until firm. Cut dough into 1-inch lengths and form into crescent shapes. Place on an ungreased cookie sheet and bake in a 325° oven for 20-25 minutes. Cool slightly on a rack and sprinkle with confectioners' sugar. Makes about 4 dozen cookies.

| Each serving provides: | | | |
|---|---|---|---|
| 365 | Calories | 33 g | Carbohydrate |
| 5 g | Protein | 236 mg | Sodium |
| 24 g | Fat | 00 mg | Cholesterol |

# Egg-Free Lemon Snowballs

*Makes 8 Servings (3 cookies each serving)*

| | |
|---|---|
| 1 | cup milk-free margarine |
| ½ | cup confectioners' sugar |
| 1½ | cups flour |
| | Scant ¾ cup cornstarch |
| 2 | teaspoons grated lemon rind |
| 1 | teaspoon lemon flavoring |
| 2 | teaspoons vanilla |
| | Snowball Frosting |

Blend margarine, sugar, flour, cornstarch, lemon rind, and flavorings. Shape into ¾-inch balls. Bake on a greased cookie sheet at 350° for about 15 minutes. Drop a dollop of Snowball Frosting on top of each cookie.

# Snowball Frosting

| | |
|---|---|
| 4 | tablespoons milk-free margarine, melted |
| ¾ | cup confectioners' sugar |
| 1 | teaspoon lemon juice |
| 2 | drops yellow food coloring |

Combine all ingredients and beat well. Drop ½ teaspoon frosting on each cookie.

---

| Each serving provides: | | | |
|---|---|---|---|
| 460 | Calories | 47 g | Carbohydrate |
| 3 g | Protein | 335 mg | Sodium |
| 29 g | Fat | 00 mg | Cholesterol |

# Ice Creams, Sorbets and Candies

## Light Strawberry Ice Cream

*Makes 16 Servings (½ cup per serving)*

1   16-ounce container milk substitute

½   cup sugar

2   teaspoons vanilla

1   egg (separated)

1   16-ounce package frozen strawberries

In a blender, whip the milk substitute for 2 minutes. Turn off and add sugar, vanilla, egg yolk, and strawberries (including the syrup). Whip for 30 seconds, put into a bowl, and freeze for 30 minutes. In a small bowl, beat egg white until stiff. Fold into ice cream and refreeze in a plastic container with a tight lid. Makes about 2 quarts.

Variation: Blueberries, raspberries, or boysenberries may be substituted for strawberries. This ice cream makes a good pie filling also. After the initial 30 minutes in the freezer, spoon ice cream into a chilled, prepared pie shell and freeze until firm.

| Each serving provides: | | | |
|---|---|---|---|
| 82 | Calories | 12 g | Carbohydrate |
| .79 g | Protein | 29 mg | Sodium |
| 3 g | Fat | 17 mg | Cholesterol |

# Basic Vanilla Ice Cream

*Makes 8 Servings*

| | |
|---|---|
| 1 | 8-ounce container Rich's Richwhip |
| ½ | cup sugar |
| 1 | teaspoon vanilla |
| 1 | egg (separated) |

Chill beaters and bowl in the freezer for 10 minutes before starting. Whip thawed topping for 2 minutes. Add sugar, vanilla, and egg yolk, and freeze for 30 minutes. In a small bowl, beat egg white until stiff. Remove ice cream from freezer; fold in egg white and beat for 1 minute. Pour into plastic container, cover, and freeze. Ice cream will be ready in 24 hours. Makes 1 quart.

| Each serving provides: | | | |
|---|---|---|---|
| 140 | Calories | 17 g | Carbohydrate |
| .75 g | Protein | 29 mg | Sodium |
| 9 g | Fat | 34 mg | Cholesterol |

# Chocolate Ice Cream

Prepare Basic Vanilla Ice Cream recipe and add ¼ cup cocoa powder to ice cream before freezing for the first 30 minutes. Chopped nuts, semi-sweet chocolate bits, or broken cookies can also be added.

| Each serving provides: | | | |
|---|---|---|---|
| 147 | Calories | 18 g | Carbohydrate |
| 1 g | Protein | 29 mg | Sodium |
| 9 g | Fat | 34 mg | Cholesterol |

# Coffee Ice Cream

Prepare Basic Vanilla Ice Cream recipe and add ¼ cup instant coffee to ice cream before freezing for the first 30 minutes.

Each serving provides:

| | | | |
|---|---|---|---|
| 143 | Calories | 17 g | Carbohydrate |
| .91 g | Protein | 29 mg | Sodium |
| 9 g | Fat | 34 mg | Cholesterol |

# Fruit-Flavored Ice Cream

Prepare Basic Vanilla Ice Cream recipe and add 1 cup frozen fruit (drained) to ice cream before freezing for the first 30 minutes. Fresh fruit can also be added, but may require additional sugar.

Each serving provides:

| | | | |
|---|---|---|---|
| 147 | Calories | 18 g | Carbohydrate |
| .83 g | Protein | 29 mg | Sodium |
| 9 g | Fat | 34 mg | Cholesterol |

# French Vanilla Ice Cream

Prepare Basic Vanilla Ice Cream recipe with these changes: increase vanilla to 2 teaspoons and use 2 egg yolks.

Each serving provides:

| | | | |
|---|---|---|---|
| 148 | Calories | 17 g | Carbohydrate |
| .69 g | Protein | 22 mg | Sodium |
| 9 g | Fat | 68 mg | Cholesterol |

# Basic Sorbet Recipe

*Makes 8 Servings*

3   cups fruit or vegetable purée
1   cup syrup

    or,

2   cups fruit juice
2   cups syrup

Add purée or juice to chilled syrup (recipe follows). Pour into a 9-inch metal cake pan and freeze for 30 minutes. Remove and thaw for 10 minutes; then pour into a chilled bowl. Beat mixture for 3 minutes. Scoop into paper-lined muffin cups and freeze. Yield: 1 quart.

Each serving provides:

| | | | |
|---|---|---|---|
| 000 | Calories | 00 g | Carbohydrate |
| 0 g | Protein | 00 mg | Sodium |
| 00 g | Fat | 00 mg | Cholesterol |

# Sorbet Syrup

*Makes 8 Servings*

Combine water and sugar in a small saucepan. Stir over medium heat until sugar is dissolved. Do not let mixture boil. Pour syrup into a mixing bowl and chill thoroughly. Yield: 1 cup.

Follow the Basic Sorbet Recipe and use your imagination to make many other flavors using fruit juice, fresh or thawed fruit, and vegetables.

---

Each serving provides:

| | | | |
|---|---|---|---|
| 000 | Calories | 00 g | Carbohydrate |
| 0 g | Protein | 000 mg | Sodium |
| 00 g | Fat | 00 mg | Cholesterol |

# Frozen Fudge Bars

*Makes 8 Servings*

1    8-ounce container milk substitute

½    cup sugar

½    cup cocoa powder

1    teaspoon vanilla

1    separated egg

Whip the milk substitute for 2 minutes. Add sugar, cocoa, vanilla, and egg yolk. Beat for 30 seconds. Freeze for 30 minutes. In a small bowl, beat egg white until stiff. Add this to the frozen mixture and refreeze in popsicle containers until firmly set.

---

Each serving provides:

| | | | |
|---|---|---|---|
| 115 | Calories | 19 g | Carbohydrate |
| 2 g | Protein | 33 mg | Sodium |
| 5 g | Fat | 34 mg | Cholesterol |

# Frozen Banana

*Makes 2 Servings*

1    large banana
2    ice cream sticks
½    cup semi-sweet chocolate bits (melted)
     Chopped nuts

Cut the banana in half crosswise. Insert ice cream sticks in cut ends. Cover with plastic wrap and freeze. When frozen, remove wrap, dip in melted chocolate bits, and roll in nuts.

---

Each serving provides:

| | | | |
|---|---|---|---|
| 371 | Calories | 43 g | Carbohydrate |
| 6 g | Protein | 3 mg | Sodium |
| 24 g | Fat | 00 mg | Cholesterol |

# Chocolate Fudge

*Makes 6 Servings*

2    cups sugar

2    tablespoons cocoa powder

¼    cup corn syrup

½    cup milk substitute

2    tablespoons margarine

1    teaspoon vanilla

In a saucepan, mix sugar, cocoa powder, and corn syrup. Cook over moderate heat, stirring frequently, until a soft ball forms in cold water or registers 230° on a candy thermometer. Remove from heat and add margarine and vanilla. Cool this mixture. Beat until dull. Pour into a greased dish and cut when firm.

---

Each serving provides:

| 365 | Calories | 80 g | Carbohydrate |
|---|---|---|---|
| .54 g | Protein | 70 mg | Sodium |
| 6 g | Fat | 00 mg | Cholesterol |

# Chocolate-Almond Marshmallows

*Makes 12 Servings*

1   6-ounce package semi-sweet chocolate bits
2   tablespoons milk-free margarine
1   egg (slightly beaten)
1   cup confectioners' sugar
2   cups miniature marshmallows
1   cup ground almonds

Melt chocolate bits and margarine over low heat. Remove and blend in egg. Add sugar and marshmallows, blending well. Shape into 1-inch balls, roll in nuts, and chill. Makes 3 dozen clusters.

|  | Each serving provides: | | |
|---|---|---|---|
| 205 | Calories | 26 g | Carbohydrate |
| 3 g | Protein | 32 mg | Sodium |
| 12 g | Fat | 23 mg | Cholesterol |

# Glazed Nuts

*Makes 4 Servings*

1    cup shelled nuts (whole walnuts, almonds, pecans)

½    cup sugar

2    tablespoons milk-free margarine

½    teaspoon vanilla extract

Combine nuts, sugar, and margarine in a heavy skillet. Cook over medium heat, stirring constantly, for about 15 minutes. Nuts should be well coated and the sugar browned. Stir in vanilla. Spread nuts on ungreased foil and cool. Break into clusters.

| Each serving provides: | | | |
|---|---|---|---|
| 310 | Calories | 30 g | Carbohydrate |
| 4 g | Protein | 70 mg | Sodium |
| 21 g | Fat | 00 mg | Cholesterol |

# Peanut Brittle

*Makes 2 Servings*

1    cup sugar

½    cup shelled peanuts, chopped

2    pinches salt

Melt sugar over low heat until golden brown. Remove from heat and add nuts and salt. Blend well. Pour onto a greased cookie sheet, thinly covering. Let cool thoroughly; then break into pieces.

| Each serving provides: | | | |
|---|---|---|---|
| 435 | Calories | 103 g | Carbohydrate |
| 2 g | Protein | 258 mg | Sodium |
| 3 g | Fat | 00 mg | Cholesterol |

# Birthday Party Treats

*Makes 6 Servings*

¾  cup miniature marshmallows (white or tinted)

⅔  cup boiling water

1  3-ounce package lime gelatin

⅔  cup cold water

½  cup prepared Rich's Richwhip

6  paper baking cups

Spray a standard 6-cup muffin tin with nonstick vegetable spray. Place about 8 miniature marshmallows in each section. In a medium-size bowl, add boiling water to the gelatin, stirring until dissolved. Add the cold water and blend well. Pour 2 tablespoons gelatin over marshmallows in each muffin cup. Chill until very thick. Meanwhile, let the rest of the gelatin set at room temperature. When thick, but not set, add milk-free whipping cream and beat well. Fill each marshmallow cup with gelatin/whipped cream mixture and chill until firm. Flatten the paper baking cups and use one as a doily under each marshmallow cup. Unmold and serve.

| Each serving provides: | | | |
|---|---|---|---|
| 84 | Calories | 18 g | Carbohydrate |
| 1 g | Protein | 51 mg | Sodium |
| 1 g | Fat | .05 mg | Cholesterol |

## Substitutions

| WHEN RECIPE CALLS FOR: | SUBSTITUTE WITH: |
| --- | --- |
| 1 cup milk | ½ cup milk substitute + ½ cup water |
| | ½ cup juice + ½ cup water |
| | 1 cup water |
| 1 cup milk (for baking) | 1 cup water + 2 tablespoons milk-free margarine |
| 1 cup milk (for yeast dough) | 1 cup ginger ale |
| 1 cup buttermilk | ½ cup milk substitute + ½ cup water + 1 tablespoon vinegar or lemon juice |
| 1 cup sour milk | Same as buttermilk substitute |
| Light cream | Milk substitute |
| Heavy cream | Milk-free whipping cream or meringue |
| Sour cream | Plain yogurt |
| | Mayonnaise + 1 tablespoon sugar |
| Cream cheese | Mayonnaise |

# INDEX